I. I iz de Macdaddy, an U iz all mi hoes

II. Westside

III. Do not diss Tupac

IV. Respect your Nan

V. Thou shalt not do drive-bys

VI. Thou shalt not commit adultery (unless she iz really fit)

VII. Thou shalt deal

VIII. Thou shalt not wear false titties

IX. Thou shalt not cover up thy batty

Da Gospel According To Ali G

4th

Fourth Estate

This paperback edition first published in 2002
First published in Great Britain in 2001 by
Fourth Estate
A Division of HarperCollinsPublishers
77–85 Fulham Palace Road,
London W6 8JB
www.4thestate.com

Written by Sacha Baron Cohen, Ant Hines,
Dan Mazer and Dan Friedman

Styling by Jason Alper

Thanks to Jamie Glassman and Samantha Loshin

10 9 8 7 6 5 4 3 2 1

WARNING & DISCLAIMER: The contents of this book are
designed to be satirical, paradoxical, humorous and just
plain funny. This book contains strong language – making
references to sex, gender, drugs, violence, race and religion
and depicts images and scenes of a sexually explicit nature.
This book is only suitable for adults who are broad-minded
and are not easily offended. The views and opinions of the
fictional character Ali G, as reflected in this book do not
necessarily represent the views or opinions of the author or
indeed his publishers. All reasonable efforts have been made
by the author and the publisher to trace the copyright
holders of the material quoted in this book. In the event
that the author or the publisher are contracted by any of
the untraceable copyright holders after the publication of
this book, the author and the publisher will endeavour to
rectify the position accordingly.

A catalogue record for this book is available from the
British Library.

ISBN 1-84115-721-X

Designed by M2.
(Tony Lyons, Nicola Hammond, Kate Stretton, David Edgell,
Duncan Youel, Philippa Baile, Jesse Simon & Teresa Nemeth)

Cover Photographs © David Scheinmann

Photographs: © David Scheinmann, © PA Photos;
© Corbis Images; © Retna; © Amanda Searle;
© Hulton Getty; © Getty Images

Illustrations by Tony McSweeney

The Watcher: Words and Music by Andre Young and
Marshall Mathers © 1999 Ain't Nothin' Goin' On But
Funking Music and Eight Mile Style Music.
Warner/Chappell Music Ltd, London W6 8BS (50%);
lyrics reproduced by permission of IMP Ltd; all rights
reserved. Famous Music Corporation USA, used by
permission of Music Sales Ltd (50%); all rights reserved.
International copyright secured.

Printed in Great Britain by Butler & Tanner, Frome

www.alig.com

Da New Testicle

Dedicated to

Notorious B.I.G., 2Pac Shakur, de West Staines Massiv and MeNan.

Keep it real

Oh shit, I forgot: and MeJulie

))) hen I desided to write dis book, in me research me discoverd a book called de bible – written by a bloke called Jason Christ and his dad. 2 say de least it woz very very boring and had absolutely no pictures and certainly no muff. It woz divided into 2 parts called de Old Testicle and de New Testicle. And dese testicles iz happarently religious and not just de normal kind dat make spunk. Checkit, people iz been fightin for millionz of years over which testicle iz de best. Me say chill – play wif dem both. Wot scholars really should be concentratin on iz de shaft. And me like to fink dat dis book will be de shaft dat will unite de 2 testicles and like King Dong bring pleasure to millionz. Me want u to fink of dis book like de bible except not a hundred years old like dat iz and not written by some geeza wif a tash and sandals. Plus if dat woz so good how come Jason Christ never wrote a sequel – after all dere woz 8 Police Academys (tho 7 werent as good as de rest coz it didnt have de bruvva who could do all de beat box. By de way do you remember de one wear he did dat noise of a machine gun – dat were good wonnit and also dat one were he gets dat blowie while he iz doin a speech, dat woz well funny, and also very clever. And de best fing about de whole series iz dat dey iz all true stories – apart from 6 where dey went to Moscow – coz obviously Moscow aint a real place). But dis book ain't about Police Academy, overwise it would be called Police Academy 9 – de Story of de Eight Police Academies, which iz hactually quite a good idea for a book, but I iz doin dis one now so me will carry on. I iz ritten a 148 words so far and I ain't gonna frow dem away. Now I iz never read a hole book and I don't hexpect u to do de same. But me still fink da written word iz a very precious fing.

Along wiv many other differences, it's da one fings dat seperate us from da animals. Well dat and shittin in our hands and eatin it. Altho Dangerous Dave has done that but he woz mashed, and he did have de munchies, so I spose dat iz alrite. Me will never forget how proud I was when me managed to write me own name for the first time. In fact, if you go round to da back of Langley Village Hall, you can still see where me sprayed it, although da paint iz now starting to fade a bit, as I done it nearly 5 years ago. Dis iz a book for everyone – sumfing dat can be picked up and read at any time, in any place – from da classroom to da courtroom. So dat iz why I iz done it in well big writing, which don't just mean much less work for me, but also means dat blind and deaf people can read it innit. So sit back, skin up a bifta and suck on me new testicle.

RESPECT

Da Ten Commandants

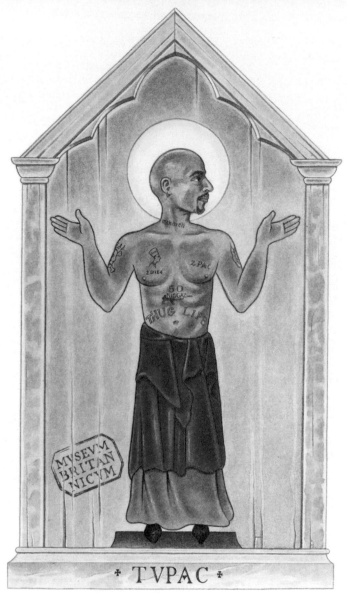

MVSEVM BRITANICVM

* TVPAC *

2 billions yearz ago a bloke called Moses climbed up a mountain in Spain and dropped 2 tablets. Dey must of been Class As coz he came down wiv some seriously mental ideaz. Dey woz called Da 10 Commandants, an dey iz de 13 laws dat has been de basis of sosiety ever since. Even de dinosaurs had to learn dem altho very few of dem hactually practisd dem an dat iz why dey died of de Aids an also why Jurasic Park appened. Ere iz wot dey say (not de dinosaurs hobviously – coz dey spoke in Dog). Also I has remixed dem for da new minellium.

Da Firs Commandant

I AM THE LORD, WHICH HAVE BROUGHT THEE OUT OF THE LAND OF EGYPT, OUT OF THE HOUSE OF BONDAGE.

As u can see coz Moses woz so mashed, a lot of dese commandants ain't even written in proper Henglish. Basically dis one iz talkin about Gad, who at de time woz de biggest pimp in de world (bit like wot Snoop iz now, except I don't fink Gad's hair was braided, even tho he woz also a bruvva). Gad woz a hero at da time coz he managed to rescue dese hoes from dis house of bondage where dey woz getting all sorts shoved up every hole – which iz out of order. So respect. Dere woz so many of dese hoes in Egypt dat dey built a massive Sphincter to which dey prayed too. Moses helped dese slags escape and on de day dey all left he performed a miracle by parting deir Red curtains. After all his hard work he woz entitled to a freebie.

DA NEW COMMANDANT
I IZ DE MACDADDY, WHO IZ TAKEN U OUT OF DE COUNTY OF BARKSHIRE, U IZ ALL ME HOES, AN IF U IZ UP 4 IT ME IZ WELL INTO BONDAGE.

Da Secon Commandant

THOU SHALT HAVE NO OTHER GODS BEFORE ME. THOU SHALT NOT MAKE UNTO THEE ANY GRAVEN IMAGE.

Dis iz a long one, so let's go thru it bit by bit. 'Thou shalt dededede…' – Dis iz basikly de 1st example of gang philosofy. Jah was a Crip, Jason Christ woz a Blood, an he iz sayin don't ever switch sides or u will get smoked. Also de second line iz about not overdoin it wiv de gravy. Let me give you an hexample from me own hexperience. On 12 May 1993 a geeza whose name shall remain nameless[1] defected from de West Staines Massiv to de East Stains Massiv. 3 weeks later he was cyclin along on his Grifter an suddenly de chain came off which led to his trousers becomin very oily and also covered in mud. Coinsidence? I don't fuckin fink so. Dis woz de work of de gods who woz well eggy at him for breakin de 2nd commandant.

DA NEW COMMANDANT
WESTSIDE.

Da Fird Commandant

THOU SHALT NOT TAKE THE NAME OF THE LORD IN VAIN.

Nowadays dis meanz do not diss Tupac or use his name in a joke (even if it iz a shaggy dog story) coz he iz dead an dat ain't funny.

DA NEW COMMANDANT
DO NOT DISS TUPAC.

---

1. His name woz Laurence Sassoon

Da Fort Commandant

REMEMBER THE SABBATH DAY TO KEEP IT HOLY. ON THE SEVENTH DAY THOU SHALT NOT WORK.

ven Jah realised dat it iz important to chill after u iz had a big Friday nite. Dis iz a well important commandant so to make sure me obeys it, me don't work de rest of de week neither.

DA NEW COMMANDANT

REMEMBER EVERY SECOND FRIDAY IN EVERY MONTH COZ DAT IZ WHEN ME HOLD DE JUNGLE ALL NIGHTA AT DE CROOKED BILLET IN IVER HEATH – 5 SQUID ON DE DOOR, FIRST 1000 LADIES FREE.

Da Fif Commandant

HONOUR THY FATHER AND THY MOTHER.

ets remember dat dis woz written in very primitiv times when people hactually knew who deir father and mother woz. Fankfully we has come a long way since den and most dads iz responsible enuf to do a runner as soon as deir kids iz born Dat iz why my new commandant iz...

DA NEW COMMANDANT
RESPECT YOUR NAN.

Da Sixf Commandant

THOU SHALT NOT KILL.

obviously u shouldn't ever kill anyone ever (unless of course dey iz called ya mum a slag, or unless u habsolutely has to do a drive-by and all your mates iz goin and it looks like it will be a larf). But killin for de sake of it iz almost alwayz wrong. Also dis dont include small birds and hanimals dat can be killed very easily wiv even de most basik airgun. Also many of de chickens dat u eat in KFC are dead by de time dey get to your mouf, and I don't wanna scare u, but a lot of dem has been killed. Most of dem by de Colonel himself.

DA NEW COMMANDANT
THOU SHALT NOT DO DRIVE-BYS

Da Sevenf Commandant

THOU SHALT NOT COMMIT ADULTERY.

Adultery meanz shaggin someone elses bitch. Hobviously it don't refer to recievin a blowie or shake 'n vac. It woz well easy not to commit adultery back den becoz most girls woz mingaz and tit jobs had not been invented.

DA NEW COMMANDANT
THOU SHALT NOT COMMIT ADULTERY (UNLESS SHE IZ REALLY FIT).

Da Eighft Commandant

THOU SHALT NOT STEAL.

In ancient times dey hactually believed teefin woz bad. Dis iz becoz no one could be arsed to nick stuff back den coz dere woz no stereos or videos (it woz only in da 15f sentury dat de Betamax woz invented). In fact in olden dayz dey only had dirt to nick[2].

DA NEW COMMANDANT
THOU SHALT DEAL.

Da Ninf Commandant

THOU SHALT NOT BEAR FALSE WITNESS.

In English dis means you shouldnt lie. Hobviously dis don't apply to wen u iz in court, coz if u dont lie den u iz gonna get sent down innit. A way to do dis moraly iz to put your hand behind your back and cross your fingaz – becoz Jah can see dis coz he iz everywhere, but de judge cant. Other times when it iz ok to lie iz when u iz comitted adultery, stolen, or done a murder.

DA NEW COMMANDANT
THOU SHALT NOT WEAR FALSE TITTIES.

Da Tenf Commandant

THOU SHALT NOT COVERT THY NEIGHBOUR'S ASS.

Dis iz basikally sayin u cannot be a battyboy, witch iz a bit hypocriticalist coz Jason Christ himself used to hang out wiv dem 12 blokes all de time[3]. My neighbourz ass iz fukin massiv deres no way I'd want to covet it. If u iz readin dis Mrs. Snaith at numba 38 I aint talkin about your batty I iz talkin about number 42 – she iz got a massive one.[4]

DA NEW COMMANDANT
THOU SHALT NOT COVER UP THY BATTY.[5]

2. Dere iz some evidense to suggest dat dey did have shitty radios back den like sanyo.
3. Dese blokes used to be called 'The Young Disciples' and play jazz-funk. Dey had a number 12 hit in 1989 wiv 'Happarently Nuffin'. By de way Carleen Anderson if u iz readin dis would u be intersested in breakin commandant no. 7 wiv me?
4. If u iz readin dis Mrs Frankelstein I iz hobviously talkin about Mrs Snaith's humungus battycrease. But I didn't want to right it in big coz den she would read it and feel upset in her heart.
If u can read small Mrs Snaith den we both know de bit above aint true an I iz just tryin to make Mrs Frankelstein feel better. She iz a bit weighed down at da moment – coz of her massive arse, aiii!
5. Dis do not apply to blokes.

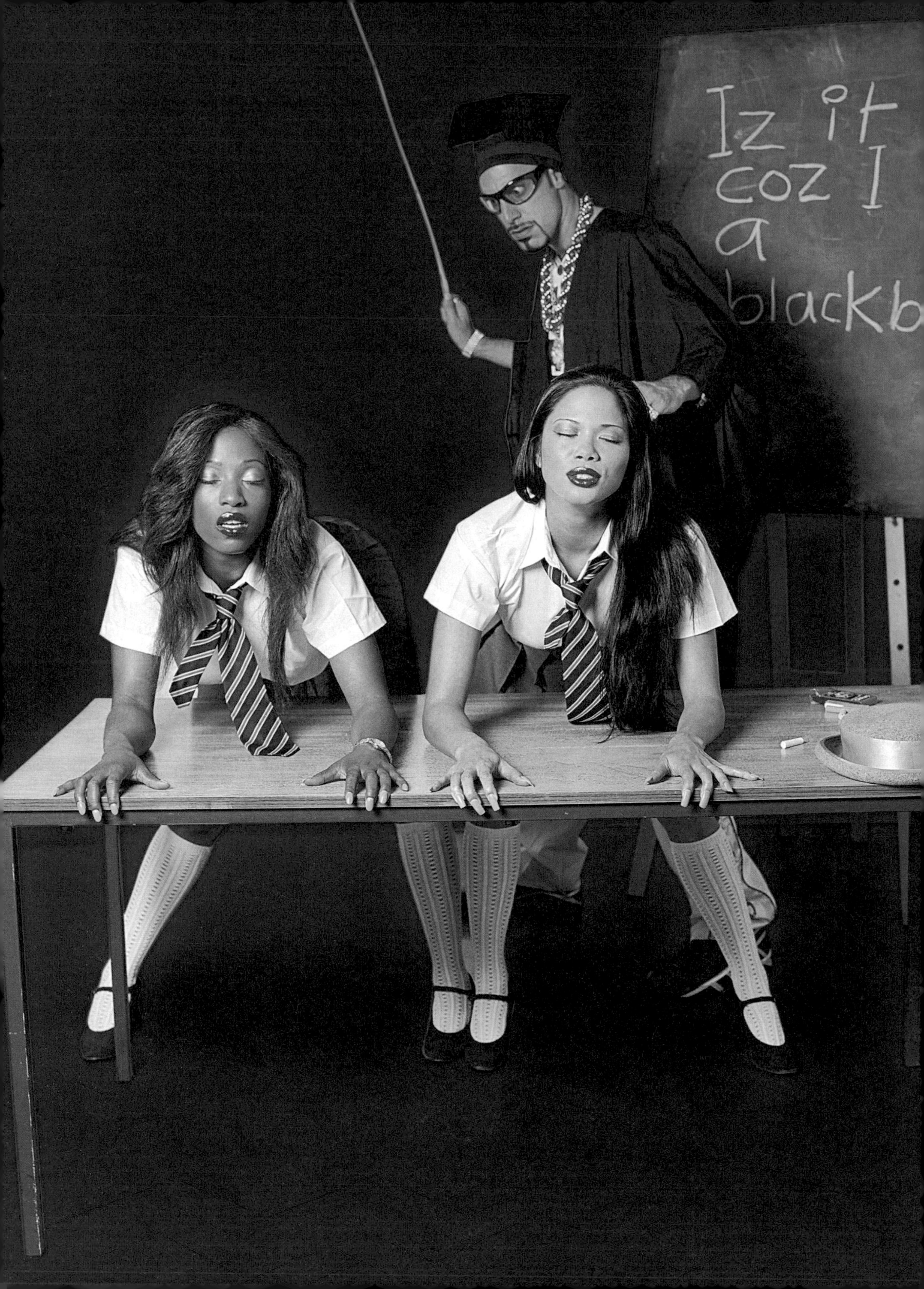
Iz it
coz I
a
blackb

Heducation

HEDUCATION

WHEN PRESIDENT BLAIRS HELECTED HIMSELF INTO DA WHITEHOUSE IN 1987, HIM SAID DAT HIS FOUR MAIN PRIORITIES WAS HEDUCATION, HEDUCATION AND HEDUCATION. FIRST OFF ALL, DAT IZ A FICK FING TO SAY, COS DEY IZ ALL NEARLY DA SAME FING, AND FIRDLY, ALTHO HEXAM RESULTS IZ BETTER, ATTENDANCES IZ UP AND STANDARDS IZ HIGHER, HE AIN'T IMPROVED NUFFIN AT ALL ABOUT HEDUCATION.

Just like da kids off today, me was failed by da skool system and I hated every single minute I spent in da classroom. In fact, added all together, dat time was probly da most borin 3 hours of me life (although me still keep in touch wiv me classmates and goes to a skool reunion every second Monday in Staines Jobcentre). But heducation iz important and skool days can be de best days of your life – after all when else iz u gonna be surrounded by 16 year old girls where everyfin iz so firm.

Dese dayz even tho me now works mostly on da telly, me do still care about heducation in Staines and me spend a lot of me time hangin around ouside of skools in da area, makin sure da kids iz spendin deir pocket money wisely, aiii.

Most of u out dere aint as heducated as me, I know u shouldn't show of, but me has got 3 CSEs. Well me hasn't hactually got dem, but me has taken dem. And to be honest me fought dey woz well easy, and just coz me and de hexaminers had diferent points of opinion, don't mean dat I woz necessarily wrong.

Even if u do take exams and don't do so well, dat ain't no problem coz you can just lie on your CV or change de letters. Like Marcel Beremblutt him woz well good at caligrafy and did joined up about a year before everyone else – for 20p he would take your report card and change 'F's to 'A's. What de membaz of de government readin dis should realise, iz dat de only real way to improve exam results iz to let everyone pass, wotever deir answers iz – let's not be racialist – just becoz people has habsolutely no inteligents does not mean dat dey should be made to feel fick. De only fing u can tell from exams iz if someone has worked hard or iz clever. Wot definitely should happen iz dat people who iz fick should have deir marks bumped up coz dey iz at a disadvantag.

TELLY DA BEST TEACHER IN DA WORLD

Dere iz many better ways off gaining knowledge dan by learnin fings and it seem mental to me dat skools even hexist anymore when da best teacher in da hole planet can be found sittin in every front room in da country for 25 hours a day, 368 days a year. You probly fink I'm talkin about your nan, but I ain't – all you'll learn from her iz dat people piss more when dey get older and dat often de best tashes can be found on women. I iz hactually on about da telly. Dere ain't nuffin dat you can't learn by watchin it and fanks to da start off Channel 5 and Granada Men & Motors, programme quality iz higher dan it iz ever been. If you picks what you watches carefully, da telly can learn you heveryfin on da National Currycolum to a standard as high as degrees or even CSEs. To save you da bovver of doin it yourself, I iz worked out a guide to wot fings on telly you should watch to get a good heducation.

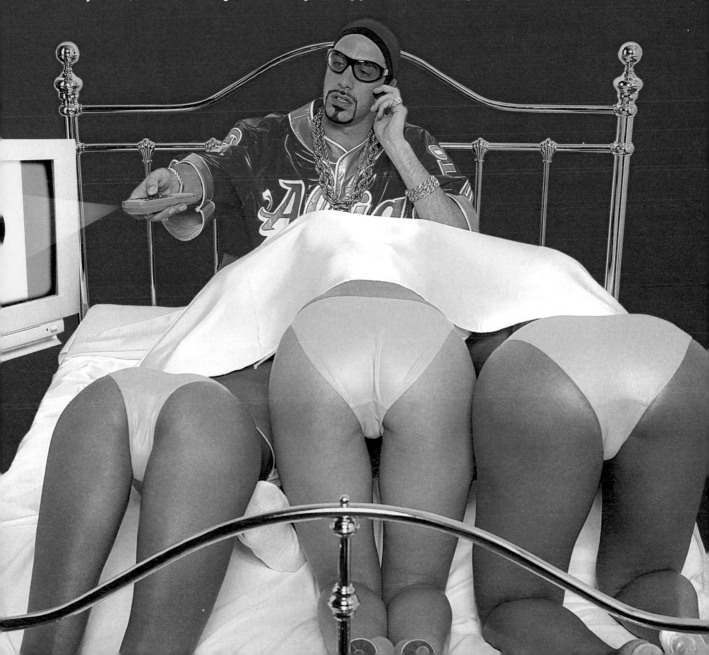

EASTENDERS

Dockumentaries like dis can learn u a lot off different fings, for hexample:

GEOGAPHRY – from studyin da map off Manchester at da start.

MAFFS – from seein how many pieces of froot da geeza wiv da Aids puts in a bag when someone say, for hexample, "me want 3 happles please".

CRIMEWATCH

As far as heducation goes, dis iz probly one off da best all round fings dat you can watch. Some of de crimez iz so sofisticated dat dey give de viewer ambition – one day if dey do a good enuf crime dey too might be able to get on da telly. Ere iz just a few off da fings I iz learnt from de programe.

MAFFS – It iz taught me dat for robbin say about 5 grand u iz likely to go down for about 2 yrs and if u rob say about a million u goes down for only 4 years more, which mean robbin a million make about ten times more sense dan robbin 5 grand.

ISTRY – Me's learnt dat if u hasn't been nicked for somefin u iz done within 2 years, den u has probly got away wiv it.

GEOGAPHRY – I iz found dat if u iz goin to do a crime, den da best place to do it iz da Wales cos deir Police iz so fick dey can't even speak Hinglish.

METALWORK – Crimewatch has taught me dat it iz possible to pick da lock of a 5 series Beama by using a simple tool dat u can make out of a coathanger and da ring pull off a coke can.

SCIENCE – I has learned dat D&A iz somefing dat iz found in da bogies off all human beins and dat when coppas look at it thru a microwave, dey can read your name and address.

Oh yeah. It would be rong not to big up and pay respect to Jan Dildo who lost her life in a reconstruktion she did for de show. U iz wiv Tupac now. Respect.

DA NATIONAL GEOGAPHRIC CHANNEL

Dis channel iz mainly soft porn and iz probly one of da best places to see free muff outside of da intranet. Watchin it u will learn amazing fings about de 3rd world – like dat bras aint been invented yet. Also on de rare hocassion when dey aint showin human babylonz, den u can watch animals doin it which iz useful if u aint got any other material in da house, coz if you squint den a gorilla can look like a girl wiv a very overgrown muff.
Dese iz da other sort of fings it teach u about.

BIOLLERGY – U can find out dat every single creature in da hole world, like jellyfish an spiders an penguins and lions all gets jiggy an dat even cats does it doggy-style – dat iz amazin. In fact dis channel iz very good to observ new tekneeks for doing it wiv your lady, I learnt a reel good trick from watching a hippo, dat made mejulie have one like she had never had before.

GEOGAPHRY – It show you dat da jungles and forests iz well shitty places and dat da West ain't doin enuff to help cut them down and build fings like McDonalds for da people who lives dere.

DA FANTASY CHANNEL

Most people probly fink dat da Fantasy Channel iz only good for teachin you fings like how to be a plumba or a telly repair man. Although it iz good for both of dese it also learns you other stuff as well.

MAFFS – I iz learnt dat 1 + 1 = a twosome, 1 + 2 = a freesome, 1 + 3 = a four-header and dat 1 + 4 = 5 squid xtra.

LANGUIDGE – from watchin Da Fantasy Channel I iz learnt to speak all 3 words of da Swedish langwidge – Inga, Helga and fliegenarschstinke. I iz also pretty sure also dat de word 'no' don't hexist in Swedish.

GEOGAPHRY – I iz found out dat that compared to da rest of da world, English girls – even slags – iz well frigid.

BIOLLERGY – At school me was told dat men only slept wiv women. Dis iz bollox, it iz also possible for dem to knob donkeys, dogs and goats.

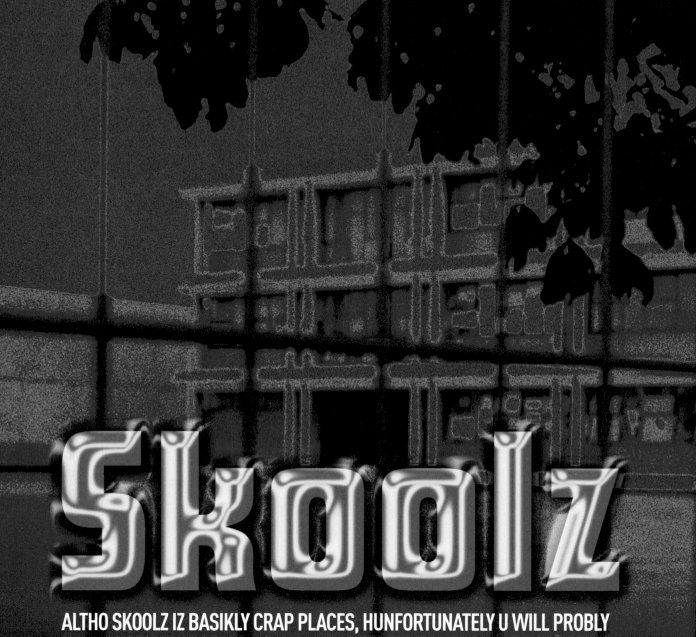

Skoolz

ALTHO SKOOLZ IZ BASIKLY CRAP PLACES, HUNFORTUNATELY U WILL PROBLY HAVE TO SPEND AT LEAST A FEW WEEKS OFF YOUR LIFE IN DEM, NO MATTER HOW GOOD U IZ AT SKIVIN. BECOZ OF DIS, U MIGHT AS WELL MAKE DA MOST OFF IT AND FOCUS ON LEARNIN SKILLZ DAT WILL BE USEFUL IN DA REAL WORLD. SKOOLS IZ INTENDED TO BE PLACES WHERE IDEAS AND IMFORMATION IZ HEXCHANGED AND IT IZ AMAZIN WHAT U CAN LEARN IN DA CLASSROOM IF U AIN'T DISSTRACTED BY DA TEACHER.

DA BEST CLASSROOM IZ DA PLAYGROUND

Altho me has been bangin on a bit about fings u can learn off of de telly, me want to point out dat da time u spend at skool can be very impotent for gettin heducated innit. Da playground iz a hole world of hopportunity:

GANG SKILLZ – One off da few ways dat skools serve dere local connumities, iz by providin a place for kidz to meet other kids in order to form gangs. Also if a kid at skool show signs of bein a badass gangsta da auforities iz helpful enuff to hexpel him so dat his nollidge gets shared around all da other skoolz in da area.

FIGHTIN SKILLZ – Da world iz a very violent planet and for parents of puny kids it iz a comfort to no dat skoolz iz a safe place to send dem to get beaten up on a daily basis. Me don't support bullyin in any way (even tho it can be a wikid larf) but at skool it make a lot off sense to developp de fightin skillz u will need later to survive in da ghetto, by duffin up kidz who iz a lot younger and smaller dan u iz.

DEALIN SKILLZ – Da playground iz long been a place for kids to developp dealin skillz wivout havin to worry about gettin victimized by da Fuzzy Muff or smoked in a drive-by. Although dey iz mostly just swappin Pokermon cards or floggin nicked mobiles, me has herd some encouragin reports dat more and more children in da skoolyards of Barkshire iz hactually tradin da erb.

BONIN SKILLZ – Every single skool in da country have at least one girl who act as a 'bonology teacher' to da boyz and iz more dan happy to give dem all a bit off 'private tuition' in her classroom – which iz usually behind da wheely bins. When me woz at skool, it woz a girl called Tracy Burke who provided dis service. Altho she iz now 29 years old and ways 19 stone and iz got 4 kids, me here she iz still more dan happy to help out any 14 yr old boys who iz strugglin in dis subjeckt.

Skoolz iz good for some tings

Here iz me advice on makin da most off all da different subjecks:

HENGLISH

Me has never been hable to c da point off teachin someone a languidge dat dey already speak. Why don't we just teach kidz American – dis languidge iz really spreadin fast and even people on de other side of de Atlantic iz beginnin to talk it.

Da only fings me can fink Henglish lessons can be useful for teachin iz dese:

IMPRESSIN GIRLS –

A quality girl likes a long word almost as much as she likes a long dong. So ere iz some well long words dat u should slip in –

1. **'Computer chip'** – use dis wen u iz talkin about computers or da intranet. For hexample:
Her: Allo I iz very interested in techmology Ali.
U: Well I iz interested in it too Sandra. Did u know dat a example of techmology iz a computer-chip.
2. **'Fowl play'** – whenever u say dis it will himpress da girl.
Her: Do u watch much tellevision Ali?
U: No, I do not becoz of de foul play.
3. **'Laboratory'** – very good when u iz with posh girls
Her: I love science Ali.
U: Wotever, I iz got a tortoise head, could u direct me to da laboratory.

Feel free to try dese at any time an me guaranttee it will get u some.

DE TUPAC TIMES TABLE

MAFFS

Da majority of fings dey tell u about in maffs, like percentages, fraktions, subtractin, minussing, addin and plussin, iz just feories dat no one really knows iz true or not. For all of u teachers out dere dat iz usin dis book as a teachin aid, me has invented a better way of teachin kids deir times tables. It iz called: DE TUPAC TIMES TABLE.

1 X 2PAC = 2PAC MAY HIS NAME BE PRAISED
2 X 2PAC = 4PAC MAY HIS NAME BE PRAISED
3 X 2PAC = 6PAC MAY HIS NAME BE PRAISED
4 X 2PAC = 6PAC MAY HIS NAME BE PRAISED
5 X 2PAC = ERM...AHHH...ERRR...I AIN'T A COMPUTER CHIP
6 X 2PAC = I KNOW DE ANSWERS TO DESE OBVIOUSLY, SO WHY
          DONT U FILL IN DE REST SEEIN AS U IZ SO CLEVER AT ADDIN UP
7 X 2PAC = ...MAY HIS NAME BE PRAISED
8 X 2PAC = ...MAY HIS NAME BE PRAISED
9 X 2PAC = ...MAY HIS NAME BE PRAISED
10 X 2PAC = ...MAY HIS NAME BE PRAISED

CHEMMISTRY

Dis iz another subjekt dat don't really have anyfin to do wiv da real world, cos it involve messin about wiv fings dat only hexist in da laboritry, like oxygen and H_2O. Dere iz a few fings it can learn u tho:

1) DE RECIPE FOR SUPASKUNK

2) HOW TO MAKE AN EXPLOSIVES – da equation for makin a bomb iz surprisinly easy: ALL DA FINGS IN BOTTLES + ALL DA FINGS IN JARS = A BOMB.

3) GEMETIC ENGINEERIN – dey don't teach u dis til Btec. Dey iz now developt de techmology dat enables a tomato to be grown from seedz.

4) CLOMING – dis means dat u can make loads off copies of de same biological person. It iz like takin a Bustarhymes cd and makin many tapes of it, except wivout de hissin. Dere woz a couple of clomes in my skool when I woz growin up, one woz called Alan Lambert and de other woz called Phil Lambert and I always fought dat dere woz sumfin well weird about dem coz dey woz hexactly de same – de same face, de same hair, de same eyes, de same everyfin. And check dis DEY even had de same birfday – how do u hexplain dat?

TW9 ROD

Phyziks may sound like de most boring subject in da world – after all who needs some teacher tellin u fings u already know, like dat fings falls downwards if u drop dem. Howeather, phyziks will prove to be da most useful subject for life in da ghetto. For hexample, it would be himposible to start a car engine without knowin about de phyzics of otwiring. And if it wern't for phyziks how would any self-respectin gangsta know how to disarm an ADT burglar alarm.

Me has learned many other fings from dis subjekt:

HELECTRICITY – me learned in phyzics dat helectricity make people generous. All u iz got to do iz put da two wires on someone's balls and dey will hand over dere dinner money.

NUCLEAR – if u ever come in contact wiv a nuclear bomb and has to dimantle it den NEVER EVER EVER EVER EVER HEVER cut de red wire – dis will set it off – go for de blue one first, and if dat don't work den go for de red one.

REFLEKTIONS – phyzics taught me dat if u drops a mirror carefully on da floor, usin da laws off gravity, it will den allow u to study various colours of da rainbow, dependin on wot knicks da girls iz decided to wear dat day.

Da male Genitalz   Da Female Flangr

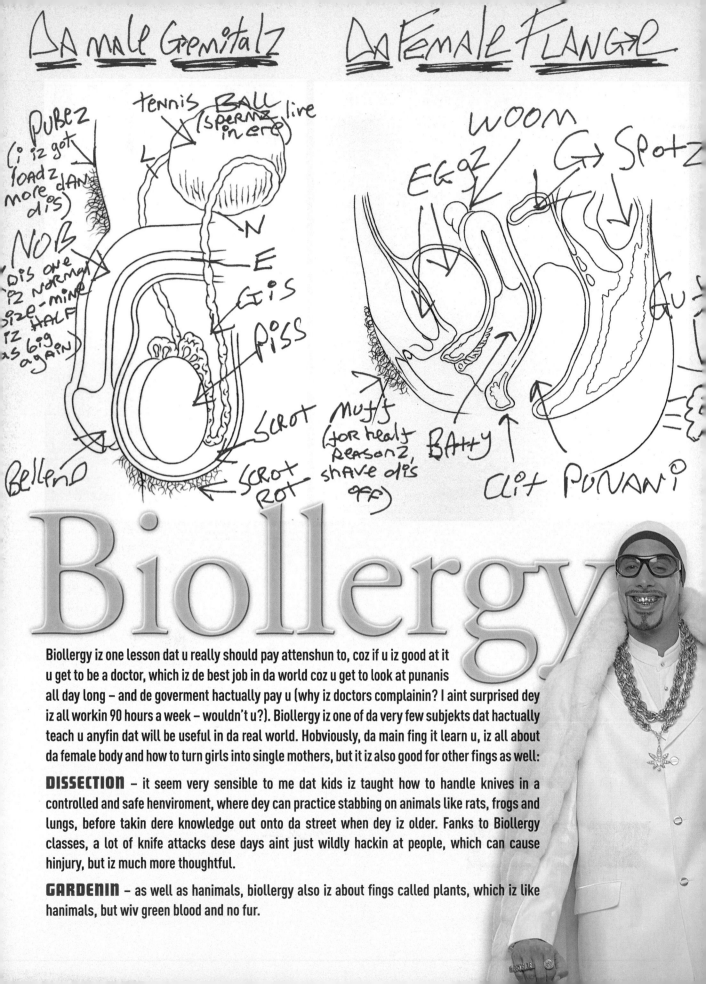

PUBEZ (i iz got loadz more dan dis)

tennis BALL (spermz live in ere)

L

N

E

GIS

PISS

NOB (dis one iz normal size - mine iz HALF as big again)

Bellend

Scrot

(Scrot Rot)

Muff (for healt reasonz, shave dis off)

WOOM

EGGZ

SPOTZ

CU...

BATTY

Clit PUNANI

Biollergy

Biollergy iz one lesson dat u really should pay attenshun to, coz if u iz good at it u get to be a doctor, which iz de best job in da world coz u get to look at punanis all day long – and de goverment hactually pay u (why iz doctors complainin? I aint surprised dey iz all workin 90 hours a week – wouldn't u?). Biollergy iz one of da very few subjekts dat hactually teach u anyfin dat will be useful in da real world. Hobviously, da main fing it learn u, iz all about da female body and how to turn girls into single mothers, but it iz also good for other fings as well:

DISSECTION – it seem very sensible to me dat kids iz taught how to handle knives in a controlled and safe henviroment, where dey can practice stabbing on animals like rats, frogs and lungs, before takin dere knowledge out onto da street when dey iz older. Fanks to Biollergy classes, a lot of knife attacks dese days aint just wildly hackin at people, which can cause hinjury, but iz much more thoughtful.

GARDENIN – as well as hanimals, biollergy also iz about fings called plants, which iz like hanimals, but wiv green blood and no fur.

PHYZICAL HEDUCATION

Phyzical Heducation iz probly resposnible for making more gaylords in dis country dan any other fing (apart maybe from house music). Fink about it, if it weren't bad enuff havin to wear plimsols and dem white vests, dey den make u get into da shower together in da nude. As well as encouridgin battyness, dis also iz very cruel for boys who iz got small dongs – although dis hobviously didn't affect me, and me woz never larfed at or called, 'Smally G', or 'Ali Tul Cock'.

To help make sure dat u or your child does not have to do it – ere iz an hexcuse letter dat I iz used for many years.

Dear sir/Miss/Lezza,

me sun iz very very ill – he iz got a well itchy skrot and it u makes him go in da showaz wiv da other boyz den dey will get it to innit – not dat he wood ever tink of touchin dere nobz – he woodunt ever do dat in a millin yearz coz he iz very very mesculin and iz got a beast dat iz well in hadvance of hiz age. And dat aint all – he iz only gone and got himself a fuckin veruka and it u iz wondrin why he aint brought in hiz rubba sock – dat iz coz he uzed it 4 somefin he shouldent have done. (in da musik storeroom wiv Claudia Lister behind da chellowz last Fursday – by da way me dont fink she'll be doin PE for a wile eitha). I hope u iz well and me no dat dem haccusationz of u bein a kiddy fiddla aint tru (wink wink). Afta all, i iz sure dat Mattew Maclean needed to be taught da correct way off dryin himself wiv a towell when naked.

Yourz sensirely

~~AAE NAN~~ Nana G

GEOGOGRPHY

Dis iz well important so dat u know de differense beween Eastside and Westside. Geogaphry iz a good fing, coz wivout it dere would be no turf wars – and no one wants dat. In case u iz an ignoranus here iz a map of da world:

LEGOLAND

NORVEN ISLAND

ISLAND

DA SOUTH PE

AMERICA

U.K.

BRITTUN
ENGLAND
WALES

STAINES

DE FROZEN FOOD TRADE

EASTSIDE   WESTSIDE

USA

HAMSTERDAM

DE CHICKEN TRADE

DE DRUGZ TRADE AND
DE PORN TRADE

ICELAND

JAMAIC

DA BLACK SEA

KENTUCKY

DANGER!
DE BERMUDA TRIANGLE

SOUTH CENTRAL

HAMPTON

→ Tupac lived here
(an me rekkon he probly still does)

SWEDEN

...N TRADE

...LAND
...TH POLE

No swimmin ere coz dese iz floataz

UNDISKOVERD TERRITERY

DE TAKEAWAY TRADE

WORLD OF LEATHER

DA NEW PLANET OF DE APES

DA OLD PLANET OF DE APES

DE UM BONGO TRADE

CHINA

JURASSIC PARK I

(Dis ain't as good as 1 & 2)

JURASSIC PARK III

Dis iz a giant turd dat iz uninabidable
by human beins and only flies lives dere.

JURASSIC PARK II

CONGO

(I iz drawn in de nuts — dey ain't
hactually a country in case u woz
finkin of movin dere).

BANGLADESH

WATERWORLD

CYPRUS
Cyprus Hill

De Channel
Tunnel

DISNEYLAND

ART

ART IZ ANOTHER SUBJEKT DAT IZ WELL IMPORTANT – AND NOT JUST COZ MOST ART TEACHERS IZ QUITE FIT. HEAR IZ MY SEKTION ON IT.

WOT IZ ART?

Art iz a well good subjeckt becoz u can say anyfin iz art. U could do a shit on a table and instead of getting a detension for it u can just say dat iz art.

VanGog woz de most briliant artist ever coz when he woz colurin in he never went over any off de lines.

Annuver reason to study art iz dat u can do any old rubbish and some posh idiot will pay billions of squidz for it. Look at dis for hexample: Dis iz supposed to be someones face. IT IZ RUBBISH. It ain't realistic at all. How old do u fink de person who drew dis woz? 4 years old? 5? No, he woz about 30!!!

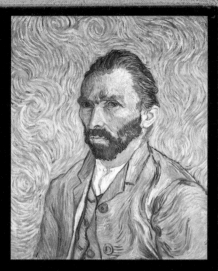

Wot do u fink his job woz? A plumber? One of dem blind geezas who tune pianos? No – he woz a profesional painter!!! U wot. Yes, I ain't shittin u.

De best painter ever woz a geezer called Tony Hart. He created not only Morf but also Mr. Bennet. A Hart if sold for auction could fetch somewhere in de region of 2 to 3 billion squidz – especially if it woz one dat took a long time to do wiv string and eggboxes and cotton wool.

HOW SHOULD U LOOK AT ART?

U should always focus 2-3 inches behind de painting, an stare really hard wifout blinkin, an den u will see de real picture – it will probably be a spaceship, or a dolphin, or a dragon, and it will be in 3D, which means u will see it in two dimensions.

WHAT IZ DA HARDEST FINGS IN DA WORLD TO PAINT?

(try and paint dese – I dont fink u will be hable to)

Water... wait for it... in a glass bowl (coz it iz see-thru, but u still have to draw it, an if u colour it blue it looks rubbish). **De wind** – and you're not allowed to use flagz. **De dark. A bullet. Fantasy Someone whose fist iz in one place an his face iz in another place** – but his fist iz made of glass. Wait for it... an u can see a reflection of his fist... in his fist!
A paintin of a paintin. A paintin of a paintin of a paintin.

It'z hobviously impossible to paint a picture of yourself. Coz u cannot be in front of de painting and behind at de same time – unless u iz clomes (see biollergy).

FRENCH

French iz a subjekt dat teach u da diffrent languidges off Europe like German or Spain. It aint no point learning dem tho, coz apart from Brittun, all da other countries iz now got rid off dere own languidges and instead speaks a new one dat iz called Euro which iz like da Inglish dey speak in America. French iz also well important to learn coz as we all no, French girlz iz not only fit, dey iz also some of de biggest slags in Europe. Respect or should I say 'Respaux'

Here iz some French words and fraises guarantteed to help u get some:

Je mapple Ali – hello, my name iz Ali

Je mange le ginge minge – I like ginger pubes
(definitely use dis if she iz got ginger eyebrows)

Je habitte in Staines – I live at me nan's

J'aime le chip de computer – I like de computer chip

J'aime le Piat D'Or – Me like de fine wine. Dis one iz guarantteed to get u some coz it proves dat u iz classy

Other wordz dat mean de same in both languidges are:

Café – café

Piscine – use as in Hinglish 'finish your homework and stop piscine around'.

MUSIC

Dis don't teach anyfin about music cos it iz always taught by old people dat do not even no da diffrence between jungle and ragga. Even tho he was old, Mr Cloolow new dat I was gifted an every Fursdy after skool in da secund year me an three uvva gifted boys would dress up in swimmin trunkz and look at his gas mask.

CHEATIN

De only fing dat u can ever tell from exams iz dat someone has worked hard or iz clever. Dat iz why de only real way to pass dem iz to cheat.

METHODS:

1) Get a chip – not like fish and chip stupid – and stick it in your head, den get your mum at home to type in de answers on her computa. Dese will be transmogulated into your brain.

2) De biggest cheatin method of all iz 'revisin' before the exam. Dis method involves workin out de type of questions dat mite be arksed and memorisin all de revelant hinformation. Dis method iz favored by spods and girlz.

Altho me don't need 2 proof how
brainy i iz, ere iz sum proof......

THE MATTHEW ARNOLD SCHOOL — TERM REPORT

STUDENT: Ali G	ATTENDANCE: 63 4%
SUBJECT: Chemistry	EFFORT / COMMITMENT: B
YEAR / STREAM: 5R	ATTAINMENT: DA BESSE

Dis iz so good me hasn't had to change it (not dat i'z changed anythink else ever)

PERFORMANCE:

Whilst curiosity and initiative are usually qualities to be encouraged in the young mind, Ali's constant refusal (and sad inability) to follow the simplest of instructions regarding safe laboratory procedures, has given me no option other than to exclude him from taking part in practical experiments. Following the no doubt unpleasant experience of having his stomach pumped on two occasions, perhaps in future he will believe me when I tell him that swallowing Nitric Acid (however dilute) will not, infact, enable him to fly, and that you cannot synthesize the compound "Ecstasy", by mixing together elements whose chemical symbols combined, spell that word.

Dis iz bollox — me hadmit ta acid didn't work — but me did hactually make hecstacy

TEACHER'S SIGNATURE: Dr.G.R.Chapman.

THE MATTHEW ARNOLD SCHOOL — TERM REPORT

STUDENT: Ali G.	ATTENDANCE: 115%
SUBJECT: English	EFFORT / COMMITMENT: Eksellent
YEAR / STREAM: 4 rem	ATTAINMENT: A

PERFORMANCE: Ali has an <u>insatiable</u> appetite for both the spoken and written word. Unfortunately, he expresses the former solely through expletives and inanities and the latter by scrawling on desks, walls, floors, ceilings — in fact, anywhere other than in his English exercise book.

As far as Ali's reading skills are <u>concerned</u>, he's taken the <u>initiative</u> of substituting books officially part of the <u>syllabus</u> with publications of his own choice. Again, unfortunately, The Oxford Local Examinations Board do not currently test pupils' <u>knowledge</u> of texts such as 'Razzle' and 'Barely Legal'.

Dese iz all hexsellunt kwalities to be told dat u have innit.

TEACHER'S SIGNATURE: HOF Alvarez

THE MATTHEW ARNOLD SCHOOL — TERM REPORT

STUDENT	Ali G
SUBJECT	Mathematics
YEAR / STREAM	4. rem
ATTENDANCE	~~43~~ 5%
EFFORT / COMMITMENT	E *iz VERY clever*
ATTAINMENT	U *da bomb ALi*

PERFORMANCE: Despite the fact that I've only had the pleasure of Ali's company on ~~three~~ *four* occasions, since he was moved ~~down~~ to the ~~remedial~~ *BRAINIEST* Maths group, he's still managed to establish himself as one of the most memorable pupils I've ever had the ~~misfortune~~ ~~boo~~ to teach. His interest in this subject goes no further than him finding it increasingly amusing each time he hears me say 'number one' or 'number two'

TEACHER'S SIGNATURE Mrs. F. Cox.   *Find dis → cum on! evryone fuany innit*

THE MATTHEW ARNOLD SCHOOL — TERM REPORT

STUDENT	Ali G.
SUBJECT	Physical Education
YEAR / STREAM	
ATTENDANCE	98% (Participation 2%)
EFFORT / COMMITMENT	EMAZIN
ATTAINMENT	FLIPPIN EMAZIN

PERFORMANCE: For someone who constantly boasts of their male prowess, it baffles me why Ali should so regularly find himself "accidentally" in the girls' changing rooms.

Also, despite on a few occasions failing to provide a reason excusing him from a PE lesson, he has, to my knowledge, only once been prepared to them take a shower with the rest of the boys. Admittedly, certain ~~lewd~~ *jellus* remarks from a few of them are probably a factor here, and it may be helpful to reassure Ali that not all boys 'develop' at the same rate.   *Dis iz true — me woz FAST and hactully had pubez at da age off 15*

TEACHER'S SIGNATURE D. Norton.

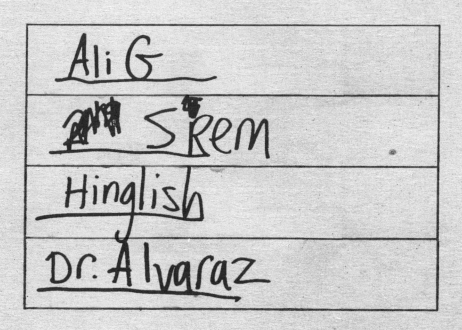

| Ali G |
| S Rem |
| Hinglish |
| Dr. Alvaraz |

alig

alig   alig

alig   alig   Alig

          ALag

          aLig

A STORY BY ALI G

Good start it iz 1983 And de vietnams war iz still goin strong coz America iz just in hawaii. Al ~~all~~ ~~itz~~ tanks distroyed in an harbour by dis massive pearl necklace dat woz brought about by ~~itz~~ tousands off JAPS Eyez. De world iz cookin 4 a new Hero and dat ~~a~~ Hero iz me and his name iz .... **ALI G**. Checkit i'm a coppa And a nutta. Me woke up dis ~~morning~~ afternoon an i woz stuck in dis prison wif ~~3 5 7 8~~ 9 spys— only ting iz dere iz a twist — dey iz female girlz an well fit. me get it on wiv dem (it iz tasteful — None of dem iz MINGAZ) den me get some ~~knives and guns~~ machine guns an me kill about ~~20 90 100 300~~ 500 people, and me save de girls And dey iz more dan grateful and dey do all sorts of fings 2 my COCK. Me got dis watch an it can hexplode an dis geeza Nicks de watch and den he is tryin 2 use de stop wotch an his arm getz blown off — NASTY — And den me wake up and ~~it~~ iz all a dream, But me turn over and de girlz iz still dere. DE END

necessary detail— we wanna ou about is already l me.

Dat werent really de end me just wonted u to fink dat it woz de end. Den de Rushins come again and me have some NUNCHUKAZ. AND Dave iz in it (u know - him de fat one dat iz IN CLASS 4d) he iz de straight coppa an him play it by de book.

Den he says - "'" You fukin little commie me got $2 millin squid on dis an u went an blew it on dis'". An den dis geeza is about to shoot me an den he falls on me an den i pull of his MASK an gues wot it iz dave!

DE REEL END

ha ha ha tell it - dat werent de
end neeither. Den i look round
de room an sumfin iz STRANGe
sumfin dat just aint makin sence.
iz it de window? No it aint de
widnow coz de window iz fine
alright, PERfecktly NORMAL. iz it
de chair? No dere aint NUffiNK
funny about de chair coz it iz a
NORMAL CHair. iz it de brooom cubboard?
No, dere's NUffiNK apart from NORMAL
brooms in de cubbord wiv dust from
cleanin so ard. iz it de window?
YES it iz. it iz well
differRent 2 wot it woz
5millonfs gf a second ago. Dere iz a
white fingaless glove on de sill.
Me RUN 2 de glove and got 2 it
REALLY fast and i put me
fingaz inside de gove.
Den suddenly i couldunt have made a
worse mitstake - itz only a bleedin
magik glove from de future dat eats
your handz and BALLz. And suddenly
de glove iz SUCKING out all my BRAIN
and feelins from my HEART. DA END

said dave as he rushed en wiv de fingaz of de fingaless glove witch den started mouldin togetha. Den me took off de golve an looked at it and it said, "dis glove belong 2 king Arcfed de great and if u aint king Alfred and u try 2 put it on, u will feel skitty"

Suddenly it all made sence. And den i woke up. And me nan woz sittin dere on me bed and she sayed dis, ""Did u have a dream?"", and i said, ""Yes"", and den suddenly i look at her hand and wot do i see? Me see dat she iz wearin oncy one white glove. Coinsidense? I dont tink so.

De BEGGiNiNG

E+ Well don Ali - this is by far your best work to date.

<u>Items</u> <u>needed</u> <u>at</u> <u>Hinglish</u> ALiG

1) Exercise, readin an Ruff books

2) Ruler

3) Penis

4) Pencil and Rubba ~~JONNIES~~

5) Colored biro or crayon or flet tip

6) DO NOT WRITE IN RED

8) Do Not write in grean

9) Do Not write in purple vane

PTK

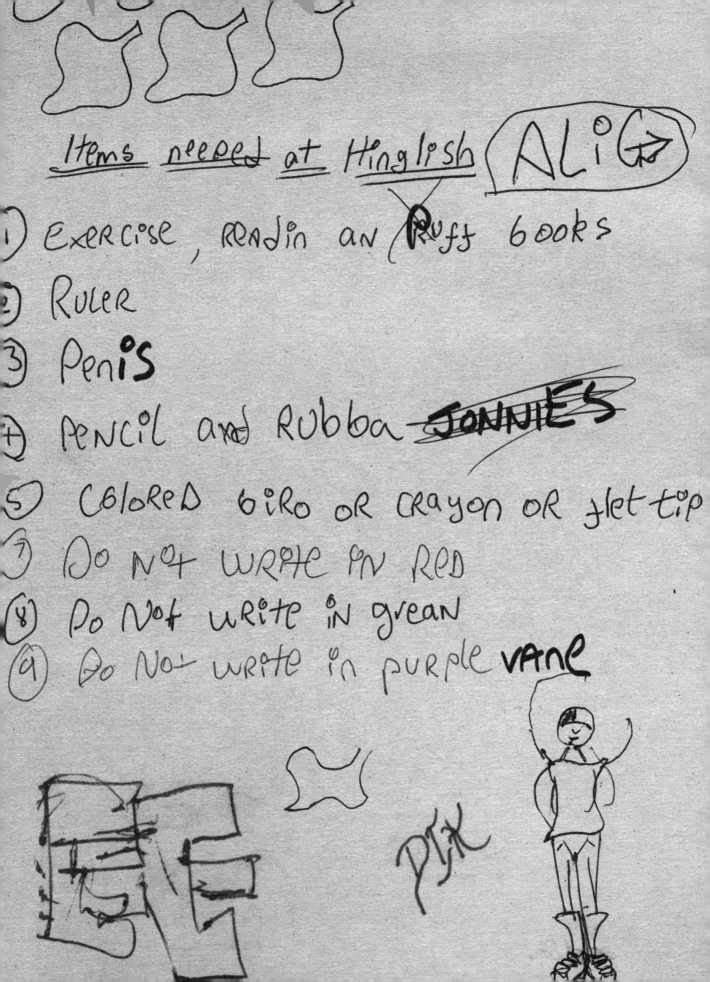

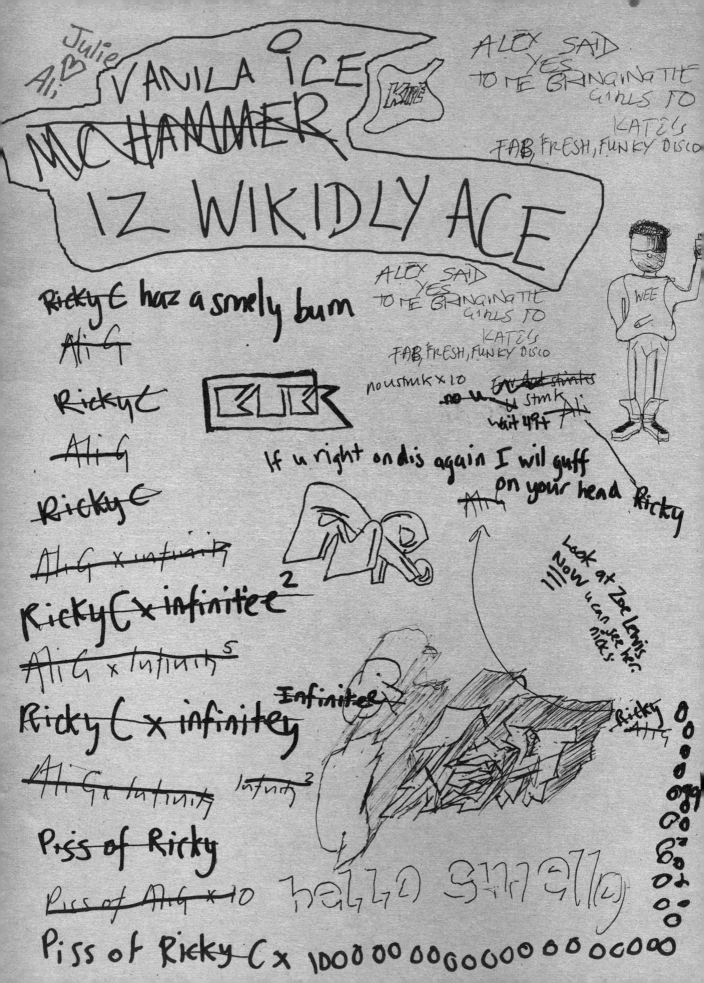

Da Well Fair State

Gouverment cutbacks dese days iz so bad dat a lot of kidz iz forced to commit crimes even if dey dont hactually need to do dem. In fact benefitz iz now so low dat some people iz even better off gettin a job. Dis dont mean dat u shouldnt still claim dem tho — fink about it — wot iz prezident blairs pay check every monf if it aint just a huge fukin giro? But gettin da dole and income support aint ezy tho — da formz u has to fill in iz dezigned to trip u up, and if u make just one tiny little mistake, dey wont send u no cash innit.

To elp u oot, iz included a felled in dole form for u in dis book. Bare in mind dat u may have to change a few fingz in it dat dont happly to u — for hexample, u will probly have to change da bit where it ask 4 your name and haddress, unless u iz also called Ali G and lives in da same house as me. Once u iz changed fingz in it like dat, den all u iz got 2 do iz cut it out and hand it in and me garantee u will get maximum benefit.

A1 claim form

INCOME SUPPORT

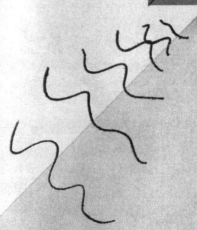

Your claim pack contains claim forms for
- *Income Support*
- *Council Tax Benefit*
- *Housing Benefit*
- *Child support maintenance*

and more information about these benefits.

You | **Your partner**

[handwritten: Do NOT admit to avin a PARTNER — it just COMPLICATE tingz]

Do you have a partner?
We use *partner* to mean a person you are married to or a person you live with as if you are married to them.

- **No** ✓ — You must answer all the questions that apply to you.
- **Yes** ☐ — You must answer all the questions that apply to you and your partner.

Does your partner agree to you making this claim?

[handwritten: STIK to your STORY]

- **No** ☐ — We will get in touch with you about this. But still tell us as much as you can about your partner.
- **Yes** ☐

[handwritten: How can me tell v about me partna when I iznt got one?]

Letters	Numbers	Letter		Letters	Numbers	Letter
N o	K i A6 3 1	0				

National Insurance (NI) number — *[handwritten: DONT tell dem your REAL one — invent one instead + u cant tink of one, den just copy some NUMBAZ and leHevs off your moBile]*

Get this from your NI number card, payslips, tax papers or letters from social security.

If you do not know your NI Number, have you ever had or used one?
- No ☐   Yes ☐ | No ☐   Yes ☐

Surname or family name — *[handwritten: If YOUR surname aint one of da 4 they iz suggested den right it in da box]*

| Mr / Mrs / Miss / Ms | Mr / Mrs / Miss / Ms |

All other names in full — *[handwritten: dis iz a well tick question — how iz u sposeo TO WRITE all other namez aport from yours in just dat LiTtLE box? PuT iN AS many AS u can]*
[handwritten: dave julie nan nicky chole jamal JPAd AvEJ JL8 pUff q jezzy davenan]

All other surnames or family names you have been known by or are using now. — *[handwritten: NONE]* *[handwritten: i iz never sined oN usiNg any over namez — incudin not usin da namez SMITH, SMALLS, evons, SHAKUR, BECKHAM or anytin else — honest]*

Include maiden name, all former married names and all changes of family name.

Date of birth | / / | / / |

Address
Please tell us your address. And tell us your partner's address, if different.

[handwritten: Me live at me nans house and i iz already told u i iznt got a PARtna innit]

Postcode | Postcode

Daytime phone number if you have one | Code Number | Code Number

Textphone number if you have one | Code Number | Code Number

You | **Your partner**

If you or your partner are homeless but have a temporary address, even if this changes from day-to-day, please tick this box
☐ Please say where we can get in touch with you in the address box below. | ☐ Please say where we can get in touch with them in the address box below.

If you or your partner are homeless and have nowhere to live at all, please tick this box
☐ Please say where we can get in touch with you. | ☐ Please say where we can get in touch with them.

Postcode | Postcode

Marital status
Tick the boxes that apply to you and to your partner.

[handwritten: TICK all dESE boxes coz it make u look well unlucky and dey mite feel SORRy for u and give u some HExTRA]

	You				Your partner	
Married ✓		Separated ✓		Married ✓		Separated ✓
Living together ✓		Divorced ✓		Living together ✓		Divorced ✓
Single ✓		Widowed ✓		Single ✓		Widowed ✓

Have you or your partner ever claimed Income Support, Jobseeker's Allowance or a Social Fund Payment?
If the claim was turned down, still tick Yes.

- No ✓ / Yes ☐ Please tell us about this below. | No ☐ / Yes ☐ Please tell us about this below.

Office that dealt with the claim

Date of last payment, if any

If you or your partner's name or address was different then, please tell us what it was.   Full name   Address

[handwritten: No Never, ever me Promise honest. Da stuff u iz got wiv my name on it at dis adress aint me. dat iz becoz me mum cAlled all me bruvvas ALi as well coz she iz a bit spasticated and she SPEAK like dis — "NEr nev NEr nev NeV". CAN me have a bit of hextra cASh please coz she CANT ASK herself.]

Postcode | Postcode

Date you moved to your present address | / / |

If you or your partner are still claiming income-based Jobseeker's Allowance we may not be able to pay you.

You | **Your partner**

Are you or your partner pregnant? → *watch out for dem tryin to trick u*

No ✓   *me hasn't got a Partna — REMEMBA?? And how can me BE PREGNANT when i iz a MAN?*

Yes ☐   When is the baby expected? / /

Your partner: No ☐   Yes ☐   When is the baby expected? / /

Are you or your partner registered blind? — *Dis Anotha trick question. Ansa it like dis*

No ☐   *Me can't reed Dis*   No ☐   *Question cos*

Yes ☐ → *i is Blind*   Yes ☐

Are you or your partner sick?
Tick Yes, if you or your partner have claimed or are getting Statutory Sick Pay (SSP).

No ☐   *iz got da aidz, da foot and mouf and dat dizease dat make soldiers from da golf war go mental*

Yes ☐

Your partner: No ☐   Yes ☐

Are you or your partner getting Statutory Sick Pay (SSP), Incapacity Benefit or Severe Disability Allowance.

No ✓ → *can me Ave it tho PLEAze*   No ☐

Yes ☐   Yes ☐

If No, have you or your partner claimed Incapacity Benefit or Severe Disability Allowance.

No ☐   No ☐

Yes ☐   Yes ☐

Dese diseazes iz worf a xtva six squid each and will also get u tree ronnies

If **you** are sick and you do not have an employer or if you are self-employed, please fill in form **SC1** *Your claim for Incapacity Benefit* – if you have not already done so – and send it to us with this completed form **A1**.

You may lose benefit if you do not provide original documents by the date on the front of this form. If you cannot provide these documents, please tell us why in Part 16.

You | **Your partner**

Are you or your partner looking after someone who is sick or elderly?

No ☐   No ☐

Yes ☐   Yes ☐

If you have answered **No** to all the other questions in **Part 2**, please use this space to tell us why you are claiming Income Support.

Be honest wiv dem — dey will respekt u for it →

coz u getz money for doin nuffink

We need to know about any work that you or your partner are doing now. Any work that you or your partner may have done in the last 9 months.

This includes
- work for an employer or self-employed work
- full-time or part-time work
- permanent or casual work
- paid or unpaid work
- paid or unpaid parental leave

Wot? stop it. Why iz u still goin on about me Julie? she ain't me partner — we haz just done a few times — well nattually LOADZ of times — but datz da benefit of havin a gf/riend innit.

Have you or your partner done any work in the last 9 months?

No ✓   Please tell us below how you and your partner supported yourselves when you were not working. Then go to **Part 5**.

Yes ☐

Be VERY carefull ere — dey iz tryin 2 trip u up.

cum off it. I ain't done a dayz work in me life. I iz survived by drinkin me own piss and eatin me mates like in dat film where dat plane crashed in to dat mountin — it woz good wonnit, altho I can't imagine me ever doin dat.

You | **Your partner**

Are you or your partner on parental leave from your employment?

No ☐   No ☐

Yes ☐   Yes ☐

Dis iz code for me sayin dat me deal a little bit. It never nurtz to hadvertise your bizniss

	You	Your partner
Are you or your partner owed any money? *InniT No* ☑	No ☐ Yes ☐ Please tell us about this below.	No ☐ Yes ☐ Please tell us about this below.
Do not include money owed for overtime.		

How much is owed? £ *15 squid* £

What is it owed for? *Dave owe it me for a teeny* — *which iz very good value i iz sure u'll Agree. if u iz intrested, me mobile numba iz 03783 905622*

Have you or your partner had any holiday pay or pay instead of notice in the last 9 months?	No ☐ Yes ☐ Please tell us about this below.	No ☐ Yes ☐ Please tell us about this below.
What was the total amount?	£	£
What date was it paid?	/ /	/ /
What date was it due to be paid?	/ /	/ /
How long was it for?	months weeks days	months weeks days

You must send us proof of the holiday pay or pay instead of notice. For example, a payslip or letter from the employer.

You may lose benefit if you do not provide original documents by the date on the front of this form. If you cannot provide these documents, please tell us why in Part 16.

Have you or your partner had any redundancy payments or lump sum payments in the last 9 months?	No ☐ Yes ☐	No ☐ Yes ☐

You must send us proof of the redundancy payments or lump sum payments. For example, a letter or statement from the employer.

You may lose benefit if you do not provide original documents by the date on the front of this form. If you cannot provide these documents, please tell us why in Part 16.

Please read the *Notes* that came with this claim form before you fill in this part of the form. → *Dis iz da only place in da hole world dat u want to admit to havin kidz — even it u hasn't got any —*

Do you want to claim Income Support for any children? No ☐ Go to Part 6.
Yes ☑ Please tell us about these children below.
Please remember you cannot claim for
• children who are boarded out with you
• foster children.

Dey iz all very nice children who well brainy and good lookin. Da girlz will probly be very fit like dese muthas and da boyz will be masta gangstaz.

Do any of the children you want to claim for have a living parent who does not normally live with you? No ☐
Yes ☐ Please remember to fill in Part 21 at the end of this form.

About the children you want to claim for

Use your imaginatoin and tink up namez dat sounds real

Relationship to you
For example, son, niece, grandchild, stepson or none.

Surname	Other names	Date of birth	
Lopez	Britney	5 / 9 / 62	me kid
Combz	Maria	5 / 62 / 9	me kid
Shakur	Biggy	9 / 5 / 62	me kid
Carey	Dave	62 / 5 / 9	me kid
Smalls	Tupac	6 / 6 / 6	me kid
Cobit	Julie	x / 14 / 10	me kid
Beckham	brooklin	8 / 7 / 88	me kid

Please tell us in Part 16 of this form
• if you want to claim for more than 7 children
• about any children who who usually live with you but are
  – in hospital
  – at boarding school
  – in local authority care
• about any foster children living with you.

(Dis kid probly iz hactually mine)

P.S. whotever u do DON'T get dis form mixed up wiv da one from da C.S.A. innit.

Does anyone live in the same house as you, who you have not already told us about on this form?

No ☐ Please go to Part 7.
Yes ☐ Please tell us about these people.

	Person 1	Person 2
Full name	ME nAN	ALI G
Sex	Male ½ Female ½	Male ✓ Female ← WOT ??
Date of birth	ABES AGO	/ /
Relationship to you	Me nAN	MESEf
Do they work for 16 hours or more a week?	No ☐ Yes ☐	No ☐ Yes ☐

Do you or your partner have any of the following?
You must answer for every item in the list.

	No	Yes	Amount
Bank accounts	☐	☐	£
Building society accounts	☐	☐	£
Post office accounts	☐	☐	£
National Savings Bank account	☐	☐	£
Premium bonds	☐	☐	£
Unit trusts, ISAs, PEPS or other investments	☐	☐	£
Money from a redundancy payment	☐	☐	£
Money from the sale of your house	☐	☐	£
Money you have saved for something	☐	☐	£
Money or property held in trust	☐	☐	£
Income Bonds or Capital Bonds	☐	☐	£
Any other money you have	☐	☐	£

u iz got a JAR off 2p's dAt iz keppt in dat fing unda da fone — u know at da top off da stairs Me Nan sayz me can have all off dem when she kick it it iz good. Me Reckon dat, wiv inflation and INTREST it mite be wort az much az 9 squid,

Shares	☐	☐	Name of company the shares are held in	Number of shares
			£		
			£		
			£		

It iz best to hadmit to havin a Little bit off money, dis wAy it look more reaL and dey wont tink u iz a Bullshitta.

How much are your savings worth in total? £ Me wone know until iz counted all da 2p's Hobviously.

If you or your partner have more than 3 types of shares, tell us about them in **Part 16.**

You must send us proof of all these savings if they are worth £2,500 or more in total. For example, your most recent bank statement or a savings account book. Bank statements must show dates relevant to the time you complete this claim form and savings account books must be up to date.

You may lose benefit if you do not provide original documents by the date on the front of this form. If you cannot provide these documents, please tell us why in Part 16.

you need to claim any of these ?
~~ase read through this list of social security benefits and~~
~~swer the question below.~~

Child Benefit ✓
Child Benefit – Lone Parent Rate ✓
Jobseeker's Allowance ✓
Earnings Top-Up ✓
Severe Disablement Allowance ✓
Incapacity Benefit ✓
Industrial Injuries Disablement Benefit ✓
Reduced Earnings Allowance ✓
Disability Living Allowance ✓
Motability or any other help with mobility problems, ✓
for example, an invalid vehicle ✓
Attendance Allowance ✓
Widow's Benefit ✓
War Pension ✓
Maternity Allowance ✓
Retirement Pension ✓
Invalid Care Allowance ✓
Guardian's Allowance ✓
any other social security benefit. ✓

← tick all dese becoz gettin a Benefit iz like gettin a Blowie — u iz got to ask aboot 50 ~~times~~ timez b4 u get Lucky innit.

Have you answered all the questions on the form that apply to you and your partner, if you have one?
If **No**, please tell us why you have not answered all the questions.
There is more information about this in the notes at the front of this form.

No ☐
Yes ☑ *0*

if u haccidently swear at dem — hapologize immediatly — dis way u keep dem sweet.

i iz ALREADY told u a million timez i aint got A FUCKIN PARTNER!! — shit, soz scuze me french dere — me didn't mean to swear at u — it iz coz i iz eggy coz me can't find a job and on top of dat i iz unemployed

Can you provide all the documents we have asked for?
If **No**, please tell us why you cannot provide all the documents.

No ☐
Yes ☐

u iz got R read between da lines on questionz like dis — even people who work 4 da dole iz on da make innit.

wot documents does u want? Me mate dave iz got a well good color printer and he can knock u up anytin u want — includin gun licenses, police I.D. cards, swimmin certificatez — anytin. You scratch my nob (not litrally) and I'll sratch yours innit.

Please use this space to tell us anything else you think we might need to know.
Continue on a separate sheet of paper, if necessary. But make sure you sign and date it and write your full name and address and National Insurance (NI) number on it.

By da way — i iz noticed dat u aint asked wot race i iz. Aint dat a bit racialist?

1. 2PAC aint dead
2. Afrika bambata woz honiginally in da soul sonik force — and not da ovver way around.
4. snakes skin iz hactually dry — and not slimey az u would hexpect.

Now read the declaration

I understand that if I give information that is incorrect or incomplete, action may be taken against me.

I understand that I may lose benefit if I have
● not answered all the questions on this form that apply to me and my partner, if I have one, or
● not provided all the documents asked for.

I understand that the information I have provided may be checked with other sources. The information may be used for other purposes relating to the work of the Department of Social Security and the Employment Service and may be given to other bodies as permitted by law.

I declare that the information I have given on this form is correct and complete.

I declare that if I have said that I want my Income Support, and any other benefits paid with it, paid into an account, I have read and understood the notes about being paid in this way.

Please sign and date this form.
This is my claim for Income Support.

Signature

Date

All u iz got to do now iz put your tag ere

Now please read the notes on the next page of this form.

For office use only

I read back to the customer the entries I made on this form based on the information given by them.
The customer agreed they were correct.

Interviewing officer's signature
Best wishes Dane Bowers

Customer's signature

Date

i iz copyed someone elses signiature ere so that they definotly has to give u some money.

GETTIN A JOB

WHEN U HEAR DE WORD CAREER U PROBLY FINK OF DAT COUNTRY IN CHINA WHERE DE VIETNAMS WAR APPEND. BUT IT IZ ALSO GOT SUMFIN TO DO WIV JOBS.

BASIKLY EVERYONES DREAM JOB IZ TO GET LOADZ OFF MONEY FOR DOIN HABSOLUTELY NUFFINK – I IZ CURRANTLY LIVIN DAT DREAM. DAT IZ WHY DE MOST SOUGHT AFTER JOBS IN TODAYS WORKPLACE ARE DOSE OFF DJ, GANGSTA, DEALER OR PIMP. PEOPLE WHO AINT CLEVER ENUF TO GET DESE JOBS BECOME LAWYERS, DOCTORS AND SIENTISTS AND HAS TO WORK WELL ARD FOR NO CASH.

A REAL GROWF AREA IN HEMPLOYMENT IS DAT OFF CRIME. MORE AND MORE YOUNG PEOPLE IZ GETTIN QUALIFIED AND JOININ 'FIRMZ' ALL OVER DE CUNTRY.

Why people iz forced to commit crime

Boredom

In da Barkshire ghettos, hapart from youf clubs, cinemas, featres, sports centraz, musement arcades, football, school clubs, go-kartin, dry-slope skiin, ice skatin, paintballin, fishin, skatebordin, Leggolandin, hoops, sea cadetz, music workshops and swimmin, dere aint nuffink for kidz to do, so it aint ardly surprizin dat dey turns to crime.

If me was da president of dis country, as well as providin fings to keep kidz off da streetz, dere iz a lot of other hobvious fings me would do to stop dere bein so much crime. Ere iz just a few off dem:

1. MAKE CRIME LEGAL.
2. GIVE ALL DA LEGAL AID MONEY TO DA CRIMINALZ INSTEAD OF DA LAWYERS, THEN DA CRIMINALZ WOULDNT HAVE TO DO DA CRIMES IN DA FIRST PLACE.
3. LEGALIZE CRIME.
4. MAKE IT NOT ILLEGAL TO DO A CRIME.
5. MAKE IT ILLEGAL TO NOT DO A CRIME.
6. MAKE IT LEGAL TO NOT NOT DO A CRIME.

Hunfortunately, at da moment me aint president of da country, so me iz unable to stop dere bein crime. Instead I iz goin to heducate you in how to commit crimes wivout breakin de law. Da first fing to fink off if u iz a criminal, iz to try and be nice about de way u nick fings.

1. If u has to break into someones property, den always leave a fanku note.
2. If u iz nickin a stereo den at least nick it from someone who uses it to listen to indie music. Dat way u iz helpin de whole community.
3. Learn from Robin Hood – he woz called dat coz he did a lot of robbin in his own hood – which cut down on travel hexpenses innit. Robin Hood later changed his name to Kevin Costner to escape de law.

Teefin da nice way

TO BE A REPUTABLE TEEF U HAS TO KNOW WHO TO NICK FROM AND WHO U SHOULDNT NICK FROM.

DONT NICK FROM

1. DONT NICK FROM YOURSELF. U aint likely to get anyfin dat u doznt already own and u will also ave to pay da cost of any damage u does breakin into your own house. On da plus side, u iz less likely to get grassed up an caught for doin da robbery.
2. DONT NICK FROM RONS SECONDHAND SHOP IN STAINES. He iz well sharp and wont buy da same stolen goods off of u twice.

3. DONT NICK FROM ME. If u iz fick enuff to even fink of robbin me now I iz earning hundreds of squids and has bought tons of dope clothes and jewellry and helectronic fings dat me keeps at me Nans house, den fink again, coz u will deffernately be caught. Dis iz because I iz installed fake security cameras and a fake halarm dat I bought from Mr. Pound in Egham. U wont even get into me Nans house now anyway, coz I iz also put loadz off extra locks on da doors and windows and hidden da keys where no one will find dem (hunfortunately, me cant find dem eiver and me an me Nan as bin lockt out for over a week now. So if u do find dem, will u let me no).

4. DON'T NICK FROM FRANCE OR EUROPE. All da fings from dese countries run on left handed helectricity, which mean dat to get dem to work in Brittun, u has to change all da wires in your house around, or paint dem a different colour, and it aint worth da assle.

5. DONT NICK MORE FISH DAN YOU CAN EAT IN ABOUT 2 DAYS. After dis time, it will start to smell quite bad. After about a week, it will start to smell really bad and after two weeks, it will smell so bad dat u an your Nan will ave to move out of your house and den da Police will come round cos your neighbours will fink dat someone iz died and den you will have to hexplain ow you got hold off da 300 boxes of Fillet-o-Fish dat iz rottin in your bedroom.

No-in da law

IF U IZ STOPPED BY DE FILTH DEN U SHOULD KNOW YOUR RIGHTS UNDER DA 5TH AMENDMENT, WITCH IS DE BASIS OF DE BRITISH CONSTITUTION.

1. U HAS DA RIGHT TO A PHONE CALL – do not waste dis on ringin Ricky C and gettin im to record Eastenders. Fink about it, use your B-R-I-A-N, it iz a waste of de phone-call coz dere iz an homnibus every Sunday innit.

2. BE POLITE – when dey ask u any questions just say 'enuf talkin about me, lets talk bout u' – dis is both polite and a good way of not tellin dem anyfin.

3. IF FOR SOME REASON DIS DONT WORK den look dem in de eye and sing 'It wasnt me' while pretendin to be Shaggy. Dey will almost definitely sing de Rayvon part and fink dat dey iz in de Notting Hill Canaveral and forget to arrest u.

4. IF FOR SOME REASON DAT DONT WORK den leg it as fast as u can. As de Olympics show u need to be on drugs to run really fast. Unfortunately for me mate Dave, bein on supaskunk dont have dat efect. He fought he woz runnin at 100mph but infact, woz crawlin on de floor, larfin and dribblin.

REMEMBR CRIME DOES NOT PAY VERY WELL (UNLESS U IZ NICKED LOADZ OFF STUFF). CONSENTRATE ON BEIN GOOD AT IT AND NOT BEIN NICKED, COZ IF U DO U WILL PROBLY END UP ON DEATH ROW.

When doin research me asked de government for figures on de amount off bruvvas on death row – dey denied de information 'claiming' dat we dont have deathrow in dis country. Cumofit. Please if u iz readin dis President Blairs hexplain de whereabouts of Musical Youth and Shakatak? I arest me case.

BRUVVAS ON DEATHROW

ARNOLD
FROM DIFF'RENT STROKES

Mr Drummond tried to defend him in court, but lost both de case and his (adopted) sons life. Willis woz devastated and had to change his name to Will Smith and iz now doin very well...

PLIERS
FROM CHAKA DEMUS AND PLIERS

Have u heard from him resently? No. Do u wanna know why? Coz he has 10 billion volts pumped thru his exit hole. Chaka Demus atended but woz unable to watch.

KELVIN
FROM EASTENDERS

DEAD for a crime he didnt commit.

PLEAZE – DONT LET DIS LIST GET ANY LONGER
[coz dere aint nuff room in da book for annyone else]

Lookin after ya money

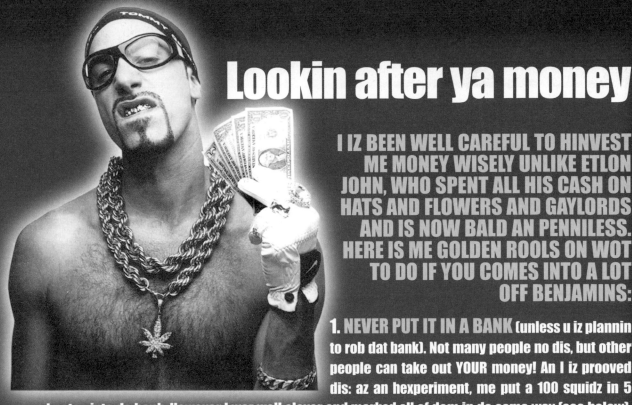

I IZ BEEN WELL CAREFUL TO HINVEST ME MONEY WISELY UNLIKE ETLON JOHN, WHO SPENT ALL HIS CASH ON HATS AND FLOWERS AND GAYLORDS AND IS NOW BALD AN PENNILESS. HERE IS ME GOLDEN ROOLS ON WOT TO DO IF YOU COMES INTO A LOT OFF BENJAMINS:

1. **NEVER PUT IT IN A BANK** (unless u iz plannin to rob dat bank). Not many people no dis, but other people can take out YOUR money! An I iz prooved dis: az an hexperiment, me put a 100 squidz in 5 pound notes into de bank. However I woz well clever and marked all of dem in de same way (see below). Den 2 monfs later when I woz checkin thru all de coat pockets in de Crooked Billet [coz I fought I had left sumfing in one of dem] me only went an found one of de hactual marked fivas dat me had put in de bank. Of course me reclamed it, coz if dere iz one fing I hate it iz teefin.

2. **CHANGE IT INTO ITALIAN LIRA** – u gets a wad off notes at least a fousand times ficker dan if it woz still in Henglish.

3. **PUT YOUR MONEY INTO GOOD INVESTMENTS** dat will retain deir value well into da future like aircuts, holidays and fashionable cloves.

4. **IF U HAS TO PUT YA MONEY IN A BANK** den become a Barclays Supasava. Coz dey iz stupid enuf to give away a free record voucher or 15 squid for free. Dey must be losin billionz of dollaz a year.

FAME!

DEY SAY DAT MONEY DOES NOT MAKE U HAPPY – DIS IS BOLLOX. IT IZ AMAZIN. ONE WAY TO GET LOADZ OFF CASH IS TO BE FAMOUS. ANUVVER WAY IZ TO BE REALLY REALLY POOR, COZ DEN U CAN SELL DE RIGHTS AND MAKE A MOVIE AN U WILL BE RICH AND FAMOUS FOR BEIN DE PERSON WHO WOZ FAMOUS FOR BEIN DE POOREST PERSON IN DE WORLD. I IZ NOW WELL FAMOUS AND DAT HAS EARNT ME MANY BENEFITS INCLUDIN VIP MEMMERSHIP AT CINDERELLA ROCKEFELLERS IN OUNSLOW.

Famous people who like me

In de last 2 years I iz met many many famous people and almost all of dem really like me and want to be my friend (includin Wyclef Jean who has said 'yo' to me when him walked past me once just like him would to a proper bruvva who hactually live in America). Here are dese stars phone numbaz. But please dont call dem UNLESS YOU REALLY NEED TO. Oh yeah and if u do DO NOT say dat u got de numba from off of me.

Madonna & Guy

001 (for America) 0301
(Hollywood) 45800149

Bono

Mobile: 007968 323225
(me don't have his hone number)

Sting

020 7004 3355

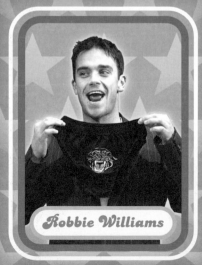

Robbie Williams

NB don't ring him after 8.30pm coz dat iz when him goes to sleep, even tho he iz almost 30 years old.
077781 167299

Prince William

Put on a posh voice uverwise u can be hung fro dis one. If u do speak to him remind him dat him still owe me 30 squid for dat stuff I gave him for his Freshers week party, aiii.
020 7004 2222

Mariah Carey

Start wiv de heavy breathing, dat will really get her goin and she'll be strummin her banjo wivin seconds.
001 031 (also America!!) 9015 3009

Woman

MAN IZ FROM STAINES

WOMEN IZ FROM EGHAM

OF ALL DA WONDERFUL GIFTS DAT JAH HAS GIVEN TO MAN, WOMAN HAS GOT TO [
RIGHT UP DERE IN DA TOP THREE, ALONG WIV DA ERB, RAPPIN, GUNZ AND KFC.

WOMEN IZ NOT ONLY DA MOST BEAUTIFUL FINGS ON DA EARTH DEY IZ ALSO USEFUL. MALES HAS BEEN ATTRACTED TO BITCHES FOR MILLIONS OFF YEARS NOW – IN FACT WE IZ BEEN KNOBBING WIMMIN SINCE EVEN BEFORE DA DAYS OF EDAM AND AVE. FROM DE MOMENT DAT EDAM PUT DAT SNAKE UP HER PUNANI – A RITUAL WITCH A LOT OF RELIDGIOUS WOMEN STILL PRACTIZE IN HAMSTERDAM – MAN SOMEHOW GOT DE IDEA OF GETTIN JIGGY. IF IT WOZ NOT FOR WOMEN DEN DA HUMAN RACE WOULD NOT BE ABLE TO CARRY ON COZ IT IZ MOSTLY DEM DAT HAS DE BABIES.

DEY CAN ONLY HAVE BABIES IF DA MAN UNDERSTANDS AND CARES FOR DA WOMAN, GIVES ER SUPPORT AND CHERISHMENT AND DEN BONES HER AT DA RIGHT TIME. DOIN 'IT' WIV GIRLS IZ VITAL FOR DA FUTURE OF DA WHOLE HUMAN RACE – EVEN IF UNFORTUNATELY IT SOMETIMES LEADS TO PREGNANCY.

WHEN IT COME TO CHOOSIN A WOMAN, U'D FINK IT WOOD BE AS EZY SEPERATING DEM INTO 2 GROUPS – DOSE U WOULD BONE AND DOSE WOODNT BONE. HUNFORTUNATELY FINGS IZ HACTUALLY A BIT M COMPLICATED DAN DAT. POPPULATION FIGURES SHOW DAT 1 IN EVE PEOPLE IZ A WOMAN AND DIS MEAN DERE IZ A LOT OF DIFFRENT TY RECOGNIZIN DESE TYPES AND GETTIN DEM TO NOB YOU IZ A SKILL LEARNT OVER DA YEARS AND IN DIS BIT OFF DA BOOK, I IZ GOIN SHARE SOME OF ME KNOWLEDGE OFF WOMAN WIV U. I IZ HAD LOADS BONIN EXPERIENSE AND CAN HACTUALLY COUNT DE NUMBER OF BITC I IZ HAD ON ONE HAND.

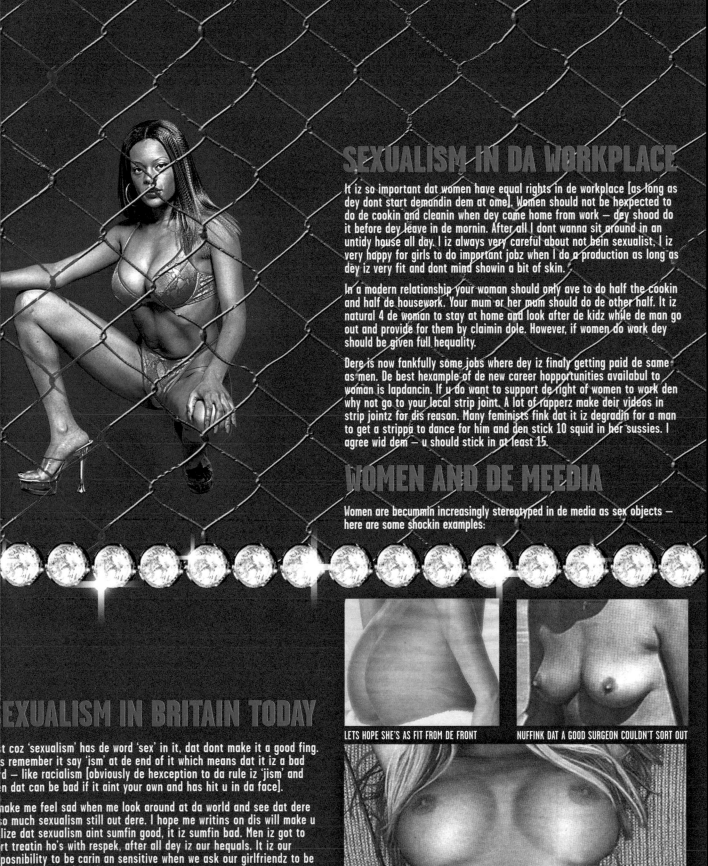

SEXUALISM IN DA WORKPLACE

It iz so important dat women have equal rights in de workplace [as long as dey dont start demandin dem at ome]. Women should not be hexpected to do de cookin and cleanin when dey come home from work – dey shood do it before dey leave in de mornin. After all I dont wanna sit around in an untidy house all day. I iz always very careful about not bein sexualist, I iz very happy for girls to do important jobz when I do a production as long as dey iz very fit and dont mind showin a bit of skin.

In a modern relationship your woman should only ave to do half the cookin and half de housework. Your mum or her mum should do de other half. It iz natural 4 de woman to stay at home and look after de kidz while de man go out and provide for them by claimin dole. However, if women do work dey should be given full hequality.

Dere is now fankfully some jobs where dey iz finaly getting paid de same as men. De best hexample of de new career hopportunities availabul to woman is lapdancin. If u do want to support de right of women to work den why not go to your local strip joint. A lot of rapperz make deir videos in strip jointz for dis reason. Many feminists fink dat it iz degradin for a man to get a strippa to dance for him and den stick 10 squid in her sussies. I agree wid dem – u should stick in at least 15.

WOMEN AND DE MEEDIA

Women are becummin increasingly stereotyped in de media as sex objects – here are some shockin examples:

LETS HOPE SHE'S AS FIT FROM DE FRONT

NUFFINK DAT A GOOD SURGEON COULDN'T SORT OUT

PERFEKTION

SEXUALISM IN BRITAIN TODAY

t coz 'sexualism' has de word 'sex' in it, dat dont make it a good fing. s remember it say 'ism' at de end of it which means dat it iz a bad d – like racialism [obviously de hexception to da rule iz 'jism' and en dat can be bad if it aint your own and has hit u in da face].

nake me feel sad when me look around at da world and see dat dere o much sexualism still out dere. I hope me writins on dis will make u lize dat sexualism aint sumfin good, it iz sumfin bad. Men iz got to rt treatin ho's with respek, after all dey iz our hequals. It iz our posnibility to be carin an sensitive when we ask our girlfriendz to be d up wiv you and her best mate.

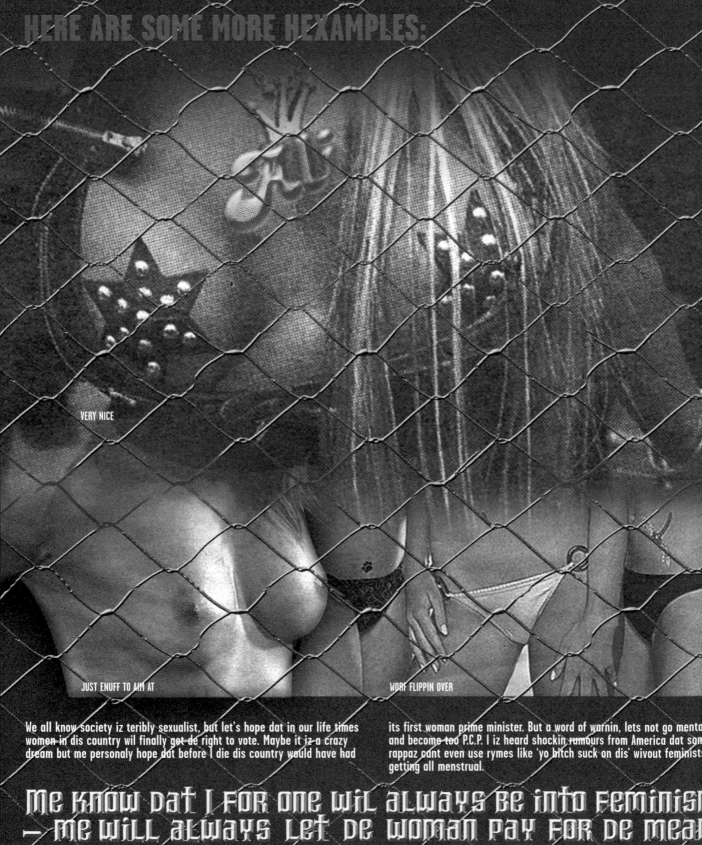

VERY NICE

JUST ENUFF TO AIM AT

WORF FLIPPIN OVER

We all know society iz teribly sexualist, but let's hope dat in our life times women in dis country wil finally get de right to vote. Maybe it iz a crazy dream but me personaly hope dat before I die dis country would have had its first woman prime minister. But a word of warnin, lets not go menta and become too P.C.P. I iz heard shockin rumours from America dat som rappaz cant even use rymes like 'yo bitch suck on dis' wivout feminists getting all menstrual.

Me know dat I for one wil always be into feminism – me will always let de woman pay for de mea, carry heavy bags and open de door for herself an me swear me will never stand up and offer woman me seat on de bus – do u know how degradi dat would be? – and I hope u do de same.

Rag Week

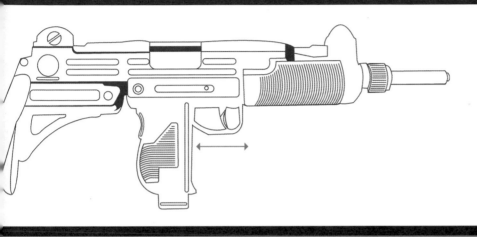

Not many people know dis but an important diference between men and women iz sumfin called 'da mental cycle' or as doctors call it, 'havin de painters in'. But no matter wot name u gives it, it still causes terrible pain and sufferin and it aint very pleasant for women eiver. Now even tho dis iz a type of 'cycle' it ain't a good one like a BMX – it iz more like one of dem bikes designed for gaylords which u fold up and has a basket on de front.

HOW OFTEN DOES IT OCCUR?

Ladies get da 'red wedge' once every 3 weeks, tho sometimes more often. Mejulie for hexample tells me she has got it at least a couple of times every week.

WHY DO THEY HAPPEN?

Medickly, wot appens iz hactually very simple. Dere iz a clock dat ticks round in her muff, when it gets to "her time" da egg dat she has been fryin in her aviary drops out of her punani.

CAN YOU HAVE INTRACOURSE DURIN MENSTURATION?

1 People fink dat you can't have sex when your lady has 'arsenal playin at home'. Dis iz not true – you can, but just not wiv her.

2 In fact u can turn de situation to ya advantage and to show how considerate and luvin u iz, suggest to her dat u do it up de wrong un.

CAN MENSTURATION HAFFECT DA WOMAN'S MOOD?

Altho hadverts on da telly for jam rags and tammys and fings like dat makes out dat women on da blob is all happy and smilin and doin sports and stuff, dis could not be furver from da truth. When it iz dere time, women hactually turns mental. It don't matter what a man say or do to dem, it iz always goin to be wrong. Remember: It iz not an easy time for your woman — be kind to her, treat her nice and try to get her to stay round at her mates.

KNOW YA BITCH...

REMEMBA WOMAN IS MORE IMATURE DAN MEN, THO DEY ALWAYS CLAIM DE OPPOSITE. I DO NOT KNOW WOT 'IMATURE' MEANS, BUT TO HELP U FURVER HUNDERSTAND DA MIND OFF WOMAN AND APPLY DIS KNOWLEGE PRACTICKLY TO YOUR RELATIONSHIPS, HERE IZ A TEST.

1 YOU COME HOME ONE NIGHT AND YOUR LADY SAYS TO U 'DO YOU LOVE ME?' WOT DO U DO?

A: say yes.

B: say 'I glove u very much' and hope she dont notice.

C: say 'I love u too' den under your breaf say 'specially deir 2nd halbum'.

D: ignore de question and ansa sumfin totally diferent – e.g. 'I believe itz called Paris. Gotta go.'

E: start to sneeze, vomit on yourself or fall over sumfin and hactually hurt yorself badly.

2 YA BITCH COMES HOME, OPENS DE DOOR AND DISCOVERS U DOIN IT SNOOP DOGGY STYLE WIV DE GIRL FROM DE NEWSAGENTS. WOT DO U DO?

A: hapologize.

B: say 'it wasnt me' in a Shaggy style voice and larf histerikly.

C: say 'I iz just warmin it up for u'.

D: u iz dead anyway, so u might as well ask her to join in.

E: turn to your girlfrend and say 'oh dis iz my mum – has u met her before, coz de one dat u finks u has met aint hactually me mum.'

3 U FANCY YA GIRLFRIEND'S SISTA. HOW DO U HACHIEVE DE 3-HEADA?

A: dismiss de hole idea. It wood be unfair on ya missus wotever her answer woz.

B: tell her dat u has notised dat her and her sista aint got nuffink in common, and dat iz why u should let her bone u.

C: arks her dis question: 'if u could stop a nucklear holocost by gettin jiggy wiv anuver woman would u do it?' If she says yes, say 'well u should keep it in da family – howzabout ya sista?' If she says 'yes', say 'shouldnt u be practisin coz u dont wanna sudenly be in dat situation and not know wot to do innit'.

D: tell de sista dat u want her to house-sit while u iz both away, but to be careful of ghosts. If she does meet any ghosts den she should bone dem. Den tell her to keep de ghosts away she must pretend to be u and speak like u and where your pijamas. Den make de room well dark and tell ya woman dat dere iz a ghost in de room and it might have tits. Den let de gamez begin.

[Tear off dis form and use it next time u wants to go out den don't leave until she has signed it. Dis will stand up in a court of law

CONSENT FORM

It is da_____day of da ___th of _____ an I iz genuinely appy dat me man iz goin out wiv his mates tonite and I aint just sayin it like I usually do and me promise not to bring it up in de next argument we has. I furver promise not to use it to force me man into coming shopin at Debenhams.

Signed. _____

4 YOUR LADY HAS JUST GONE AND GOT HERSELF A NEW SKIRT FROM TOP SHOP. SHE PUTS IT ON AND ARKS U WEATHER IT MAKE HER BATTY LOOK BIG. IT DOES, WOT DO U SAY?

A: 'no, of course not me darlin. Wot batty, me didn't even know u had one coz it iz so small and not big'.

B: start singing 'hey fatty boom boom'.

C: say 'not dat much fatter dan any ovver part of u'.

D: stay silent for a few seconds, den say 'sorry I didnt realise who u woz, I fought Roseanne woz in me bedroom'.

5 IT IZ VALENTINE'S DAY WOT DO U GET HER?

A: a dozen red roses [not plastic].

B: de new Bustarhymes CD dat u want.

C: tell her dat u iz takin her on a shoppin spree and she can buy de most hexpensive fing in da shop. Den take her to da 'Everyfin for a Pound Shop'.

D: get de most hexpensive ribbon u can buy and tie it round your helmet.

THE ANSAZ

1: 'D'.

2: 'E'. If u answered 'e' – dis will not work if de girl iz clearly much younger dan u. If dis iz de case, u should introjuice her as ya sista.

3: 'D'.

4: 'D' – coz dis iz witty she will like u even more dan she did before.

5: 'D' – dis iz wot Sir Shirley Valentine imself did.

HONEY

POSH MUFF

DERE IZ ALMOST AS MANY DIFERENT TYPES OF WOMAN AS DERE IZ DIFERENT TYPES OF ERB. AN LIKE DE SENSI EACH TYPE HAS ITZ OWN APPEARANTS, SMELL AND PRICE. DAT IZ WHY ME IZ GIVIN U SOME ANDY TIPS SO U DON'T GET SKANKED WIV SOME DODGY OREGANO. IF U FOLLOW DIS GUIDE U WILL BE GARANTEED ANY HONEY U WANT IN DA HOLE WORLD (APART FROM SPORTY SPICE AND FEMALE RUGBY PLAYAZ — NOT EVEN MY MAN TUPAC COULD HAVE PULLED DEM).

Posh girls [also known as 'IT' GIRLS coz they work with computaz] might seem out off bounds to most men, but bare in mind, Mick Hucknell has nobbed a few off dem, so dey obviously aint dat fussy. Girls like dis, who iz been well bread, aint impressed wiv men who iz too flashy and tryz to ard to show off dere money. Da suttle, tasteful approach work best.

WHAT U SHOULD WEAR:
Not too much jewlry — no more dan 8 chains and 5 rings on each hand. Old fashioned traditional cloves made of natural fibres like pollyester.

WHAT U SHOULD SAY TO DEM:
'Allo, your Ladyshit, I iz best mates wiv your bruvver — me and im was heducated at Heton together. Can me take u out for some Kentucky Fried Grouse?'

WHERE U SHOULD TAKE DEM:
Posh people love shootin so take her wiv u on your next drive-by

MUSIC YOU SHOULD PLAY DEM:
U should play dem classical music, like Grandmaster Flash or Cameo.

PRESENTS YOU SHOULD GIVE DEM:
Dis kind of girl iz only impressed wiv hexpensive fings — so anyfin from page 23 to 46 in da Argos catterlog will do.

HOW 2 GET ONE

MUSIC YOU SHOULD PLAY DEM:
Dat one from de adverts dat goes 'do-digidoo-digidoodaa-daa-da-doo-diggi-doo-dah-dah' , and den de violin goes 'da-doogida-doogid-bunbey-da-doo-deeeey-dah-dah.'
Den de paino goes really high 'digidee-digidee-dadoo-bumbey-digidoo-dadoo-daaaaa-DUM.' Dat one.

PRESENTS YOU SHOULD GIVE DEM:
Give presents dat iz food for da head as well
as da heart. Maybe a challengin game, like Pictionary.

BRAINY MUFF

Clever women alwayz wear glasses an dey don't get nuff action becoz off dat. 4 dis reason, u iz quite likely to get at least a blowie off dem innit.

WHAT YOU SHOULD WEAR:
Choose haccessaries dat say, 'iz well heducated'. One way off doin dis iz to wear a badge dat say, 'I iz well heducated'. Also wear trainas wiv laces, cos dat tell dem dat u iz clever enuff to do up your own shoes innit.

WHAT U SHOULD SAY TO DEM:
Make it clear dat u iz well brainy. Say 'I iz also well brainy' den count up to 20 for dem (practis dis before. Be careful it gets tricky around 17).

WHERE U SHOULD TAKE DEM:
Dey respect a man who happreciates computa science — so take dem to de arcades & challenj dem to Tekken 3.

MINGAZ

You can wear, say and do wotever u want wiv mingaz. Dey will be grateful for anyfin.

CCTV IN OPERATION
recorded 24 hours a day
for public safety and crime prevention

HANGIN ON 2 A HONEY

IF U IZ COME DIS FAR AND FOLOWD ALL ME TIPS U SHOULD HAVE A FIT WOMAN BY NOW. ALL U IZ GOT TO DO NOW IZ TO HOLD ON TO HER, WHICH, HUNFORTUNATELY IZ DA ARDEST FING OFF ALL. ONE OUT OF EVERY 4 WOMEN IZ MINGAZ, WHICH MEAN DAT ONLY 25% OFF GIRLS IZ HACTUALLY FIT. DIS MEAN DAT EVEN IF YOU IZ LUCKY ENUFF TO BE WIV ONE OF DEM, DERE WILL BE PLENTY OFF PEOPLE TRYIN TO TAKE HER OFF U INNIT. FOR ME DIS AINT REALLY AN HISSUE, COZ APART FROM DA TIMES ME'S BEEN DUMPED, NO WOMAN HAS EVER LEFT ME. ERE IZ SOME WAYS ME GUARANTEE WILL KEEP YOU WIV A GIRL:

1 Don't be jealous and over pocessive of her — dis will drive her away.

2 Don't let her speak to other men and if she do, threaten to kick da shit out off dem and den take her home.

3 Borrow a lot off money of her — she know dat if she finish wiv you, she ain't never gonna get it back.

4 Get her up da duff. Dis really iz a last resort.

5 Get her to wear one off dem black sacks over her clothes, like da Indus do, to stop other men fancyin her.

6 Tell her dat you iz only got six months to live (make sure dat you keep re-tellin her dis every six months, or she won't belief you).

7 Show her romantik gestures — write a love letter for her and leave it somewear were she will see it. Below iz one me wrote for mejulie on da front off da Elmsleigh Centre.

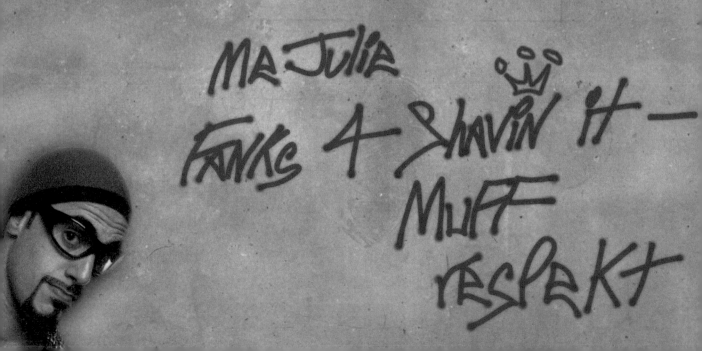

MA JULIE
FANKS 4 SHAVIN IT —
MUFF
RESPEKT

MEETING DE IN-LAWZ

IF FINGZ IS GOIN WELL U MIGHT BE FORCED TO MEET HER PARENTS AND IF U IZ UNLUCKY SHE MIGHT HAVE 2 OF DEM. HERE IZ A SIMPLE GUIDE ON HOW 2 COPE WIV DIS POTENSHALLY DISASTROUS SITUATION.

GREETINGZ

It iz important to make a very good impression.

HOW IS YOUR APPEARANCE?

Make sure u has no dirt on your cloves and none of deir daughter's pubes in your teef. When u first meet de mother be charmin and pay her a gentle compliment e.g.

'allo cheeky' and den squeeze her batty [gently]. It is a social 'no-no' to let de index finger slip into de crack area.

Next say to ya girlfriend while pointing to da mum 'I didn't know u had an hextremely younger, model sista'.

De mum will probaly say sumfin like 'wot a charmin compliment but I am hactually her mutha'.

U should imediately look surprized and say 'No fukin way – u iz sooo fit. Now me can see where your daughter got her great babylonz from.'

Den add 'If I woz really mashed I would probaly bone u'.

MEETING DA DAD

Now u iz won da mother over, try and impress da dad by showin him wot lovely times u iz had wiv his daughter.

Pull out a photo of de 2 of u together, and den say 'Dat's me and dat's your daughter. As u can see from our faces dis iz our favorite position'.

DA MEAL

Offa to elp wiv da meal. 2 make de afternoon go more smoovley add a few erbs of your own to de Sunday roast, aiii. Remember off course to always compliment da food. A perfect line wood be: 'dis desert tastes as sweet as your daughters punani'. Dis way u iz givin a double compliment innit. It iz not only important to be interested, u should also be interestin.

FAREWELZ

When u leave be careful how u answer de final question.

If de dad says:

'It has been a pleasure meeting you – my daughter is a lucky girl and I hope that one day you will settle down with her'

U should answer:

'Me can't promis u dat, but me give u me word dat I will bone her until me real bitch come back from holiday'.

VOL 864 NO 69

ALI S

G SPOT

2 SQUIDS

MISS STAINES NUDE

RIDE DE PUNANI

CELEBRITY ORGY!

BEASTENDERS!

DIS SEKSHUN IZ A DA LADIES • DO NOT LOOK AT IT IF U IZ BATTY

www.alig.com

9 786969 696966

69>

REAL PUNANI INSIDE

ALI:
DA BIGGEST BEAST IN DA JUNGLE!

Ghetto

Gangstaz

'THINGS JUST AIN'T DE SAME FOR GANGSTAZ
TIMES IS CHANGIN US NIGGAZ IS AGING'

DR DRE '2001'

ME COULDN'T AGREE WIV DIS MORE. YEAH SURE WE ALL KNOW MY MAN DRE LIKES TO HAVE A LARF, BUT HE IZ VERY SERIOUS HERE. 1 OF DE BIGEST PROBLEMZ FACIN OUR SOCIETY IS DE LACK OF A PROPER GANG CULTURE. O.G.S OR ORIGINAL GANGSTAZ LIKE MESELF IZ GOT A DUTY TO SPREAD OUR NOLLIDGE TO DE NEXT GENERASHUN OF WANNABE GANGBANGAZ.

DA ORIGIN OF GANGZ

ME WOZ BORN A GANGSTA. IT AIN'T NO COINCIDENSE DAT DE FIRST FING ME SAW WOZ DE INSIDE OF A HOPSITAL — DE 2ND HOME OF MESELF AND SO MANY OTHER GANGSTAZ. WHEN ME OPENED ME EYES AND SAW ALL DE BLOOD AND DAT DOCTOR STARING AT ME, ME JUST ASSUMED DAT ME WOZ DE LATEST VICTIM OF A DRIVE-BY. BUT NO, I HAD JUST BEEN BORN. GANGZ HAS BEEN AROUND EVER SINCE PEOPLE IS BEEN AROUND — ALMOST THREE HUNDRED YEARZ. A LITTLE KNOWN FACT IS DAT DE ROMANZ WOZ DE FIRST TO DO DRIVE-BYS, EXCEPT DEY DID DEM ON DONKEYS AND DEY HAD ONLY VERY BASIC GUNZ.

HOW 2 B A BADASS GANGSTA

HOW TO WALK LIKE A PIMP

1. KEEP WAIT ON LEFT LEG
2. KICK DA RIGHT LEG OUT AS IF U IZ AVOIDIN DOGSHIT
3. KEEP A MEAN FACE
4. SAY 'OUCH' AN LIFT YOUR LEFT LEG UP A BIT SO DAT PEOPLE FINK IT IZ PUMPED FULL OF CAPZ

INNER IPSWICH MASSIV

EAST PORTSMOUTH CREW

FORMING A GANG — GANG SIGNS

BARKSHIRE IZ RIDDLED BY A TURF WAR DAT HAS COST MANY LIVES OVER DE YEARS. IN AUGUST 1998 IN ONE SINGLE DAY DERE WERE TWO SPRAINED ANKLES AND A GRASS BURN IN A BATTLE FOR CONTROL OF DE SWINGZ IN LEACROFT PARK.

NONE OF DE GANGSTAZ INJURED WENT TO HOSPITAL FOR FEAR DAT DE FEDZ WOD GET DEM DERE.

HASSAN B (HEAD OF DE WACK BRIGADE KNOWN AS DE EAST STAINES MASSIV WHO IZ RUBBISH) HAD TO WEAR AN AFLETIC SUPPORT SOCK FOR ALMOST 3 WEEKS — AND HE'LL BE WEARIN IT AGAIN IF HE COME ANYWHERE NEAR DOSE HOBBYHORSES.

SO U CAN RECOGNIZE DEM — HERE IS DE HAND SIGNS OF BARKSHIRE'S NOTORIOUS MASSIVS AND

DE GANG SCENE AROUND DE SPELTHORNE AREA IZ EXTREMELY COMPIKATED AND DEEP ROOTED. DE HISPANIC GANGS HAVE BEEN BANGIN FOR FAR MORE YEARZ THAN ANY OF THE AFRO-BARKSHIRE GANGZ. DESE GANGZ BEGAN TO FORM AFTER DE LANGLEY VILLAGE RIOTZ IN '65, AFTER SO MANY BRUVVAS WERE THROWN IN JAIL, AND GANG WAR HAZ BEEN A PART OF LIFE IN DA PROJECTS RIGHT UNTIL DE GANG TRUCE OF APRIL '92.

CURRANTLY I IZ PUTTIN A LOT OF TIME AND ENERGY INTO 'HANDS ACROSS EGHAM', DE ORGANIZATION TRYIN TO SEE DE GANG TRUCE THRU. I IZ SICK AND TIRED OF PAYIN FOR FUNERALZ AND COUNSELIN KIDS TO QUIT SHHOTIN OVER COLORS AND TURF — LET DE KILLIN END.

2 MOST OF DE KIDZ IN DESE GANGZ, JAIL IZ NO DIFFERENT TO HOME. WORMWOOD SCRUBS DON'T SEEM DAT DIFFERENT TO ENGLEFIELD GREEN. DEY AIN'T GONNA DO NUFFIN BUT KICK IT WIV DE HOMIES IN JAIL. EVERYBODIEZ DERE. U AIN'T GOT NUFFINK ON DE STREET. SO IF U GET POPPED, SO WOT? IF YOU IZ YOUNG, U SAY TO YASELF, 'I CAN DO TWO STANDING ON MY HEAD'.

Color

DA COLORS DAT GANGBANGAZ WEARS IS VERY IMPOTENT, OR AS LENNY HENRY WOULD SAY – IT IZ 'CRUUUUCCCIIAAALLL'.

IT IZ NO DIFFERENT TO A UNIFORM DAT U MIGHT WEAR IN DA ARMY OR BURGA KING – AND IF U ISN'T WEARING DA RIGHT UNIFORM, U IS LIKELY TO END UP DEAD, SAME AS IN DA SECOND WORLD WAR, A HENGLISH SOLDIER WOULD HAVE DEFINITELY BEEN SHOT IF HE HAD BEEN DRESSED LIKE A IRAQI INNIT. ALSO IF U TURNED UP FOR WORK IN BURGA KING WIV A WIMPY OUTFIT, U WOULD ALMOST DEFINITELY LOSE ONE OF YOUR STARS.

ME ONCE WENT WIV MEJULIE TO BUY HER SOME SNEAKAZ FOR HER BIRFDAY. I PICKED OUT A PAIR FOR HER, BUT SHE POINTED TO A BLUE PAIR (COLOR OF DE EAST STAINES MASSIV) 'LET'S GET THESE.' I LOOKED AT HER AND ARKSED 'BLUE, WOT ARE U TALKIN ABOUT?'. BUT SHE WOZ LIVIN NEAR DA JUNGLE ON CEDAR'S CLOSE AND THORNTON AVENUE AND DAT'S IN DA EASTSIDE.

SHE LET ME KNOW DAT SHE'S NOT A GANGBANGA. SHE TOLD ME 'I'D RATHER JUST BLEND IN THAN TRY TO FIGHT IT'. AZ IT TURNED OUT DEY DID NOT HAVE DEM IN HER SIZE – SHE HAS A VERY WIDE FITTING, I FINK A 'G' (COINSIDENCE) SO I BOUGHT HER SOME BANGLES INSTEAD.

DOES A GANG ALREADY WEAR DAT COLOUR?

DA COLOURS OFF YOUR GANGS CLOVES TELL OTHER PEOPLE WOT CREW U BELONGZ TO AND BECOZ U WILL HAVE TO WEAR DEM FOR DA REST OF YOUR LIFE, U SHOULD CHOOSE DEM CAREFULLY. ERE IS A FEW FINGS U SHOULD CONSIDA:
IF I WOZ TO GO INTO SOUTH CENTRAL (EGHAM) WEARIN YELLOW, I WOULD ALMOST DEFINITELY GET KILLED – COZ BEIN IN DE EASTSIDE DE COLORS DERE IZ RED. WEARIN YELLO DERE IZ AS STUPID AS WAVING A BLUE FLAG TO A BULL.
AS DERE IZ ONLY TWENTY COLORS IN DA HOLE WORLD – AS PROVED BY DE SIENTIST CARAN D'ACHE – CHANCES ARE DAT THEY IS ALL ALREADY CLAIMED AND FOR DIS REASON, U WILL PROBLY HAVE TO INVENT A NEW ONE. FOR HEXAMPLE, U COULD MIX TOGETHER BLUE AND YELLOW AND CALL IT 'BLUELOW' OR MIX TOGETHER RED AND BLUE AND CALL IT 'RELUE'.

BLEEDIN

LIVES IZ SAVED OR LOST IN DA WASHIN MACHINE. IF YA SHIRT BLEEDS, SO WILL U. IT IZ ALL TO EASY TO PUT A YELLOW T-SHIRT IN WIV SOME RED PANTS AND END UP WIV EVERYFIN LOOKIN GREEN. DEN DE NEXT TIME U IZ WALKIN ON DE WRONG SIDE OF TOWN – BUKKA – U DEAD.
DAT IZ WHY DE MOST IMPORTANT FING DAT ANY GANGSTA MUST DO IZ ALWAYZ READ DE WASHIN INSTRUCTIONZ. IF IT SAY 'HAND WASH ONLY' DON'T TAKE A RISK, IT MIGHT DEFINITELY MEAN A BULLET THRU YA LEG.

TERITORY OF DE
WEST STAINS MASSIV

TERITORY OF DE
EAST STAINS MASSIV

NO-GO ZONE

SHOOTIN

DRIVE-BY

TEEFIN

DJ'IN

BURIED FINGS

BONIN

FREE CONNIES

DEALIN AN SMOKIN

CRACKHOUSE

BATTY BOYZ

FITI

LOCKIN AN POPPIN

PIRATE RADIO

LEACROFT PARK

EASTSIDE

THE ELMS
CENTRE

DA GHETTO

FITI

PART FROM THRU RAPPIN AND PIRATE RADIO AND FINGS LIKE DAT, GRAFFITI (AN KILLIN) IS DA ONLY WAY HOMIES HAS OF EXPRESSIN DEMSELVES.

LOOK AT DIS BUILDING — ITS CALLED DE TAJ MAHAL (AND I AINT TALKIN ABOUT ME UNCLE JAMALZ RESTAURANT IN BRACKNELL). IT IZ IN A TERRIBLE STATE — OVER DE PAST FEW DECADES IT HAS BEEN NEGLECTED TO DE EXTENT DAT IT AINT EVEN GOT A SINGLE BIT OF GRAFF ON IT. WIV A SIMPLE BIT OF WORK AND FOUGHT DIS STRUKTURE COULD BE TURNED INTO ONE OF DE WONDERZ OF DE WORLD — COME ON DE WEST DELHI MASSIV PULL UP YOUR SOCKS (DAT IZ IF U WEAR DEM, COZ IT IZ WELL HOT DERE INNIT?).

IT SEEM CRIMINAL DAT HERE IN DE CAPITAL OF AMERICA, NEW YORK, WHERE FITI WOZ INVENTED DAT DIS BUILDIN AINT EVEN GOT DE MOST SIMPLEST OF TAGS ON IT.

ERE IZ DE OLDEST BUILDING IN DA WORLD BUILT BY JEWIDS. FOR OVER 40 MILLION YEARZ NO-ONE HAS TAGGED IT — COME ON!

IF U AIN'T GOT ANY FITI SKILLZ I IZ GIVEN U SUM OFF MINE BY MAKIN DIS STENCIL 4 U.

PACKIN

WHEN ME TALK BOUT 'PACKIN' – I AIN'T TALKIN BOUT DE FING YOUR NAN DOES FOR U BEFORE U GO ON HOLIDAY, I IZ TALKIN BOUT HAVIN A 'PIECE'...

WHEN ME TALK BOUT HAVIN A 'PIECE' I AIN'T TALKIN BOUT HAVIN A PIECE OF CHOCOLATE OR CHICKEN (WHICH WOOD BE LOVELY). I IZ TALKIN BOUT 'GUNZ'.

WHEN ME TALK BOUT 'GUNZ' I IZ GENUINELY TALKIN BOUT PROPER REAL ALIVE GUNZ.

IT IZ ONE OF DA MOST BASIK OF ALL HUMAN RIGHTS TO BE ABLE TO ATTACK SOMEONE WHO IS DEFENDIN DEMSELVES AGAINST U. DAT IZ WHY IT IZ LEGAL TO CARRY DANGERUS AND OFFENSIV WEAPONZ IN BRITTUN – AS LONG AS DEY IS HIDDEN AND IF U IZ STOPPED BY DA COPPAS, U PRETEND DEY IS MEANT FOR SUMFIN HARMLESS.

LIVIN IN DA STAINES GHETTO, IT IZ HESSENTIAL 2 BE AWARE OF YOUR RIGHTS 2 CARRY WEAPONZ, COZ APART FROM PLACES DAT IZ MORE DANGERUS, DERE AIN'T NOWHERE ELSE IN DA WHOLE PLANET WHERE U IZ MORE LIKELY TO BE ATTACKED. FOR DIS REASON AND ALSO BECAUSE, EVEN IF U DON'T NEED DEM, WEAPONZ IZ NECESSASARY.

IT IZ A SAD FACT, BUT DESE DAYS, NO LAW ABIDIN GANGSTA OR CRIMINAL HAS GOT ANY CHOISE BUT TO CARRY A GUN – SIMPLY COS DA POLICE, WHO MAKE IT DEIR JOB OF VICTIMIZIN GANGSTAZ, IZ NOW DEMSELVES FULLY ARMED. EVEN DA TRAFFIK WARDENZ IN BARKSHIRE IZ NOW PACKIN. WE HAS ALL HEARD STORIES OF INNOCENT MOTORISTS GETTIN FIRED AT, JUST COZ DEY IZ A LITTLE BIT OVER DA SPEED LIMIT – SO FAR, NO ONE IZ BEEN HIT, BUT IT IZ ONLY A MATTER OF TIME BEFORE DEIR RADAR GUNS KILLS SOMEONE.

FACED WIV DAT KIND OF WEAPON, U HAS TO MAKE SURE U KNOWS WHERE TO GET ARDWARE OF SIMILAR QUALITY SO YOU CAN FIGHT BACK. IDEALLY, U WOULD JUST BE ABLE TO GO INTO ARGOS OR WOOLWORTHS AND BUY AN AK OR AN UZI, BUT UNFORTUNATELY DESE SHOPS DON'T STOCK DEM BECAUSE THEY IZ RUN BY DE THREE MASONS WHO IS WELL IN WIV DA FILTH.

WHY CANT WE FOLLOW DE AMERICAN HEXAMPLE? GUNZ IZ FREELY AVAILABLE DERE AND ITS NOT LIKE DEY HAS ANY MORE MURDERS OR GUN RELATED CRIMEZ DAN WE DO INNIT.

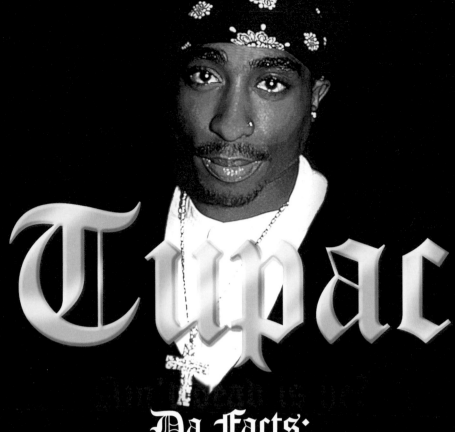

Tupac

Da Facts:

AFTER LEAVING THE TYSON FIGHT ON SEPTEMBER 7, 1996,
TUPAC WAS HALLEGEDLY SHOT 5 TIMES.

HE WOZ PRONOUNCED DEAD ON FRIDAY SEPTEMBER 13, 1996.

The suspicious facts dat prove dat he aint dead at all – not even slightly...

1. Friday the 13th is a extremely suspicious day.

2. My man Tupac oficially died at 4.03 pm.
4 + 3 = 7!!! A coincidense? cumofit.
Also he 'died' at an age of 25 yearz. 2 + 5 = 7!!!!

3. 7 x 2 = 14. Den take dat number and minus 1.
Wot do u get? 13.
Recognize dat number? Yes hobviously u do.
Ye know remember de fing about Friday de 13th.

4. Tupac's album 'All eyes on me' woz released on
Feb 13, 1996.
Tupac 'died' on Sept 13 1996. It iz quite a
coinsidence dat de two dates iz
HEXACTLY 7 months apart.

5. As if dis wosn't enuf proof me mate Jezzy F saw
him in Dixon's in Bracknell 3 months ago.
Coincidense I don't fink so. He woz buyin some

batteries. How much did dey cost?
Yeah dat's right £6.99. Guess wot he told dem 'to
keep da penny blood'.
Makin 7 squid hexactly. Fank you.

6. If u rearrange de lettaz of his album title
'Makaveli The Don Killumanati –
The 7 Day Theory' u can make de sentense 'OK
on tha 7th u think I'm dead yet I'm really alive'.
Don't beleeve me, try it yaself.

7. Wot bout dis – if u rearange de lettaz of
'TUPAC SHAKUR' u get 'u trap cak sh'
(dere is a spare 'u' which refers to de CIA
hobviously).
He iz askin us to be quiet ('sh') about de 'trappin' of
'cak', which basicaly meanz dat he couldn't 'ave
been shot, coz overwise why would he still be
tellin us dat?

Chill

healf

Dere iz a lot off crap written about food. For hexample, it iz said dat, 'u iz wot you eat'. Well if dat iz right, how come i ain't a giant chikken, wiv maybe wings dat iz made out off burgers and eyes dat look like milkshakes and Monster Munch fingaz? Oh yeah and also legs dat look like Hawaian pizza with spicy beef chunks for my toes. And hair dat look like Angel Delight?… and elbows dat iz like Findus Crispy Pancakes and ears dat iz like Birdseye Potato waffles and a massive slab of beef for a dong – hactually maybe I iz wot I eat.

Troof iz we all has to look after our bodiez. Overweightness, or osebity, iz a growing problem in dis country, specially mongst bitches and fat people. Dis mean dat people tease and iz cruel to girlz who iz a little on da chubby side. Me fink dat iz well out of order – ridicule and name calling iz da last fing fat blubbery ho's need. Names like 'fatty' 'lardy' 'fatso' 'massive batty' 'fattyboomboom' 'u iz so fat u look like King Kong' 'hitopotamus' 'fat stinkin cow' iz well out of order, and can really hurt someonez feelins, and should only be used sparingly. A good hexample of how u can help fatsos iz Grange Hill with Roland who woz so fat dat de only way dey could fit him in da picture woz to invent widescreen TV. He woz helped greatly by de sista (de one who wernt Michelle Gayle) to lose wait. I want to be dat girl for u an ere iz me 10 rules for healfy eatin.

Da ten rools of healfy eatin

1 It iz important to have a varied and balanced diet. To do dis, try to alternate between KFC, McDonalds and Pizza Hut.

2 Eat plenty of vegetables and fruit – it dont take all dat much willpower to order Onion Rings and a Hot Apple Pie wiv your burger.

3 It iz just been discovered dat eating red meat iz very bad for u. Because of dis, u should always cook burgers until dey turn brown.

4 It aint food dat make people fat, it iz da calories dat foodz contain. If u eats high fat foods, buy ones dat hasnt also had carolies added to dem by da manafaktras.

5 Try to eat diferent styles of cookin from all around da world. For a taste of da Orient me reccomend da Chinese McRib burger, or if u prefers Italian, da Chicken McKorma Nan iz both tasty and very healthy.

6 If you want snacks, try to eat Walkers 'footballer' crisps – dey iz obviously goin to be ealthier than dan non-sports ones.

7 Breakfast iz de most important meal of de day – so eat loadz off energy foods as soon as you get up at 12.30.

8 Dont eat fings dat iz been genitally modified – nobs and punanis iz full of germs.

9 Drink at least 5 litres off water every day. To make it taste better, me reccomend mixin it fifty fifty wiv Ribena or Kia Ora.

10 Try to eat foods dat iz boiled, not fried. If you dont like water, den boil fings in oil instead.

Restaurant Reviewz

57 High Street, Staines

RATINS   ★★★ | ⫚⫚⫚⫚

A small intimate place I like to go to iz called McDonalds or Maccy D's. I have met de owner, he's called Ronald. He's a funny lookin geeza (I fink he may be batty coz him got a perm and always wear lipstick) but very friendly. Since opening his first restaurant in Staines in 1987 he has now opened up McDonalds as far afield as Egham, Ruislip and even Slough.

Atmosfear

Dis popular eatery can get crowded at weekendz.

Food

I enjoyed some terrific starters ere. Try de 6 McNuggets, I reccomend de BBQ dipping sauce – itz realy tasty. De perfect drink dat I would reccomend to accompany it iz sumfin called a coca cola – which iz a cocktail de ingredientz of which r secret, and dere are only 2 people in de world who know de recipe and dey aint even allowed to fly on de same plane. Dat iz a true story.

For de main course u should look no furver dan de house speciality – de Big Mac. Dis dish has really becum quite famous around de whole area. A word of warning – de gerkin may not be to everyonez taste. If u are feelin adventurous, why not try de daily special – if u are lucky it might be de McOutback Burger with Boomerang Fries. For vegetarians de McChicken sandwich iz an excellent option. Deserts really iz de speciality of de chef at dis Staines branch. Darren dint earn his 3 stars for nuffin and his apple pies are both piping hot and delishiously crispy – I couldnt help askin for seconds.

Service

As long as u dont get Dwain (no stars) you will be pleazantly surprized – happarently he spunked in de milkshake. Service is quick, effishient and surprizinly friendly. U can have as many free straws and satchels of ketchup as u want. I cant help admittin I've become a bit of a regular. Plus de bogs iz cleaned every hour (by Dwain).

Price

For a 3 course meal without wine £2.98. Supersizing will cost u an extra 42p but iz well worth it. Booking is not essential.

If de cuizine iz not to your liking may I recommend a restaurant 4 doors down, called KFC. Owned by an ex-army officer who failed to make it into de A-team, Colonel Saunders has opened an affordable bistro specializing in chicken dishes. Enjoy.

Recipes
classic italian pizza

First take a large, roomy plate. Then ring 0114 – 323232 – when a bloke answerz
(probably Gary) say 'can I have a large Classic Italian Pizza pleez.'
Take care not to make de classic beginnaz mistake of not specifryin whether u want
fin or fick crust. Den allow 30-40 minutez for delivery. When de bell rings u will
need a sprinklin of cash and it iz sometimes nice to give a 5 – 10p tip if it iz raining.

FITNESS

BEING FIT DONT JUST MEAN HAVIN GREAT BABYLONS AND A NICE PUNANI. IT ALSO HAPPLY TO HOW HEALFY U IZ.

HOW TO BECOME FIT IF U AINT

» get silikone babylonz & visit Pink Cheeks [20 Thornton Way, Langley Village] and get a "haircut"

» get exorcised

GYMZ COST A LOT OF MONEY AND IZ FULL OF SWEATY MIDDLE AGED WOMEN, DAT IZ WHY I ALWAYZ HEXERCISE AT HOME. IF U FOLLOW MY DAILY WORKOUT YOUR HEALF AND FITNESS WILL IMPROVE LOADZ

ALIS DAILY WORKOUT

01: LIFTIN

MUSCLE GROUPS WORKED:
Biceps and triceps

It iz important 2 start your exorcise programme wiv some gentle lifting to get de muscles workin and to get de blood flowin round de body. Start of wiv very small weights – perhaps only an eighth of an ounce to start. Over de next few weeks you can build up to a half and heventualy a hole ounce.

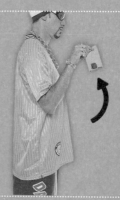

WARNING: place a mat down before u start incase any of de weight crumbles.

02: JAW WORKOUT

MUSCLE GROUPS WORKED:
Neck muscles, Upper back, Tongue

Place an object in your hand. Extend your tongue fully. Den wiv broad strokes of de head move left and right.

Once u iz masterd dis u can move on to de hadvanced hexercise, which u will need specializd aparatus for. First extend de tongue. Den isolating de neck muscles move de head up and down always remembrin to keep de tongue firm.

REPS: 20

Next while keepin tongue out, move head from side to side as if sayin 'no, me do not want to carry on anymore' which is probably true.

REPS: 20

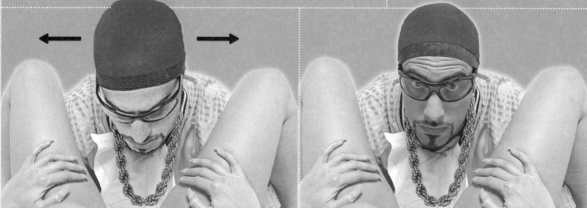

NB: de number of reps will vary dependin on how much of a slag de happaratus iz.

03: BREATHIN EXERCISES

For healthy livin it iz well important to be able to control your breavin. Take a deep bref. Hold for 10. Den exhale for 5. Repeat until mashed.

NOTE: U may feel a slight 'rush' or light headednes. Do not worry dis is normal espeshally wiv Moroccan Black.

04: FOREARM WORKOUT

MUSCLE GROUPS WORKED:
Triceps, Obliques, Extensor Retinaculun, Dong

U will find dis exorcise will soon become addictive and u won't wanna start de day wivout it. Start by puttin your arm in a right angle position. Next leavin de upper arm rigid, move de elbow joint bakwards and forwards vigorosly. It may be useful at dis point to hold onto sumfin for balance – perhaps a stick or even your dong. Start wiv gentle movementz and gradualy increase de speed.

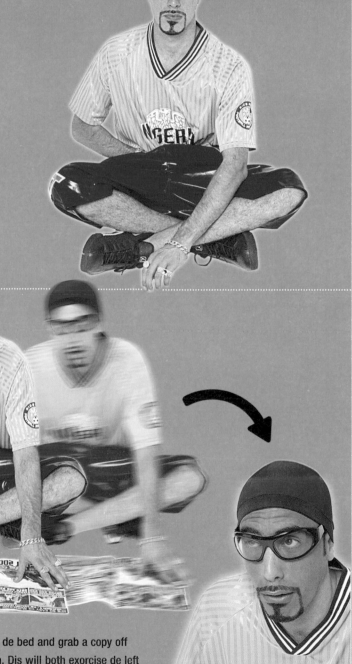

HADVANCED: With de ovver hand reach under de bed and grab a copy off Asian Babes. Next turn de pages as fast as u can. Dis will both exorcise de left arm and improve hand to eye co-ordination.

05: RUNNING

Dis may sound like a basic exorcise but it iz very good 4 fitness.

1. Find an empty street so dat when u iz runnin u will not be bumpin into people.
2. Sprint as fast as u can down it. U may need some hincentive to really push u to your limit, I find being chased by a coppa works best.
3. To increas ya fitness level try runnin while carryin a weight. Start wiv a car stereo and only when u can handle dat, hadvance to a video recorder.

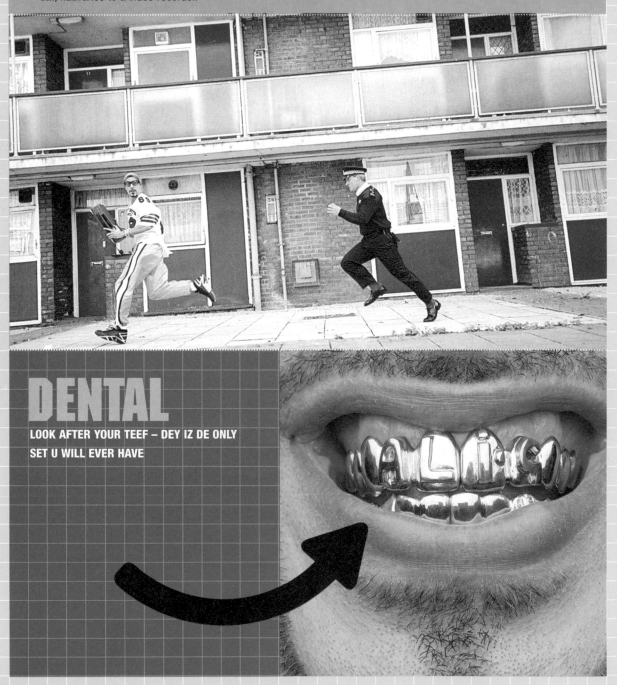

DENTAL

**LOOK AFTER YOUR TEEF – DEY IZ DE ONLY
SET U WILL EVER HAVE**

DRUGZ

Drugz dese days iz everywhere and dey always will be. Even if da auforites gets rid off all da drugz in da hole planet and stops dem ever bein made or growed again, dey aint never goin to stop people takin dem innit, so dey might as well make dem all legal and hinstead heducate people, which iz wot i iz goin to do now.

EZY GUIDE TO DA ERB

In da last 10 years, fanks mainlly to da invention of da aeroplane and super strengf batty boy connies dat don't split when they iz swallowed (an also dat bridge dey iz built under da channel between france and Europ), gettin high quality puff into da country has never been eazier.

Dis has led to dere bein at least a million diffrent types of erb havailable just in Staines alone – and altho dis iz hobviously good news for everyone – it has also caused a lot off confusion over hexactly wot u iz buyin innit. Dis iz becoz altho each type shares da scientifik name, 'erb', dey also all has dere own unique tastes and flavas – in da same way dat chicken tastes diffrent to meat even tho they iz both made of food.

To elp u walk thru dis minefield wivout gettin your head blown off, I iz done da next bit off da book as a handy guide to da erbs off da world for u to pull out and keep. Da photos in it will elp u to recognize most of da varities off puff dat iz currantly on offa in Brittun's playgrounds, prisons and rehab clinics. Relax.

TYPES OFF WEED

 **AFGHAN TALIBANGA**

 **NEVER NETHERLAND**

 **TERMINAL 5**

 **KINOBI BATHROBE**

 **TIBETAN CAKI**

 **GOAN CARWASH**

 **ETHIDOPIAN**

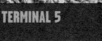 **MANALI HAND GRENADE**

 **CORIANDER**

 **NEPALESE TRAINCRASH**

 **SENSI KRONJE**

 **MORROCANE**

 **FANI BATA**

 **CHRONIC BOOM**

 **HAY BALE**

 **CHERTSEY MONGOL**

 **GRAND KENYAN**

 **FELA KUTI**

 **POOLEY GREEN RIGHTEOUS**

 **GEORGE BUSH**

TYPES OFF HASH

BAMBALACHA SQUIDGY	BATTY CAKKI	SHEMSHEMET SPEEDBOAT	PRAWN DANSAK	GRECIAN 300
OBE ONE KINOPI	EZRA POUND	GHOBI ITCH	LANGLEY HAND PRESSED	DELHI DHUNG CAKE
SOMALI STOOL	STANWELL HEADFUKKA	POL POT	KURDISH UZI	ENGLEFIELD BROWN
MALAWI GHANG BHANG	ETON BRICK	K F SENSI	GRIM REEFER	XXX

ATTENSHUN! PLEASE CHECK DIS ALSO...

As well as bein able to recognize all da genuine types off erb, u should also no dat dere iz some evil people out dere who iz floggin fings dat aint drugz. Only last year, Ricky C's little nephew had to go to hopsital afta smokin wot turned out to be owl shit dat he bought off some geeza on a school trip to Windsor Safari Park. Ere iz some off da fings dat i iz personally paid for in da Staines area. Me knew all da time dey werent genuine and bought dem just to get dem off da streetz.

OREGANO

To find out if dis iz fake weed, u iz just got to smell it. If it remind u off pizza, it iz probly oregano. Avin said dat, Warren at Egham Pizza shed (u know da smelly bloke wiv da ponytail) will hactually put a sprinklin off skunk on your pizza for a hextra tenner, so be careful not to get confused.

RUBBER BRICK FROM A SWIMMIN POOL

It iz easy to test dis one. U just drop it and if it bounse it iz hash and if it dont it iz rubber.

COW FOOD

Da only reel way off testin dis iz to find a cow and see if it want to eat it. If u see cows dat iz lyin down, dis probly means dey iz been sold fake cow food dat iz made from hash.

DANGLEBERRYS

Even tho dese iz bits off dried shit from a dogs arse, dey iz hactually quite hard to tell apart from genuine cannerbis rezin. U shouldnt worry to much about dis tho, coz dangleberrys iz hactually quite a nice smoke.

weedz of da world

To furtha advice u, i iz now goin to let you in on one off me monthly erb tastin sessions dat take place round me nan's house once hevery 3 weeks when she go to get her bag changed. Me use dese hoccasions to sample some off da new releases available from around da world and rate dem for da benefit of others.

Today me will be tastin one hexample of puff from each of da five continents of da planet ad ratin dem in terms of flava, strengf, kwality and overall value for money.

Key to Da G Erb ratin system

FLAVA	STRONGNESS	KWALITY	
Gourmet flava - unbeatable	Maximum heffect	✹✹✹✹	Fubu
Very nice indeed		✹✹✹	Nike
Acceptable		✹✹✹	Adidas
Taste it if u has to		✹✹	Reebok
Hunacceptable	Habsolutely no affect	✹	Hi-Tec

1. JAMAICA

SOMALI LAKBAY DIVA 1997

Growed in a small part off Jamaica called Somalia, it iz a miracle dat dis weed even hexists, coz it aint rained in dis part off da world for over 3 hundred years. Dis give da leaf a crisp and dry texture and make it a fast burner. It also make it very good value, wiv a quarter pound often weighin as much as 3 ounces. Fresh, floral and surprizinly smoky on da palate – i iz gettin flavas of peach, strawberry, blackcurrant and butterscotch Angel Delight. Very nice heveryday puff – ideal for drivin on.

18 Squid/eightf   ✹✹✹

2. INDIA

BOMBAY FUELTANK 1985

U can be pretty certain dat erb from dis part off da planet is goin to be kwality, just by lookin at its climate, soil conditions and da high numba off unemployed people dat live dere. Aromatic nose, full bodied and a pleazant hint of Diesel at da finish. Highly reccamended.

20 Squid/eightf  ✹✹✹✹

3. EUROP

EASTSIDE HG 2001

Growed in Barkshire by certain membaz of da ESM – It iz crap like dis dat iz preventin Brittun from bein considered a serious producer of erb on da world stage. Harsh on da palate, puny flavas and a dogshitty nose – me can fink off nuffink good to say about it.

15 Squid/eightf ✹

4. CHINA

BANGKOK COLONIC 1990

ERB OF DA MONF ☆☆☆☆☆

Me was bowled over by dis cheeky little smoke. Rich nose, wiv complex haromas of Hot Apple Pie, Turkish Delight and a elegant finish – you can ardly taste at all dat it has been half way round da world stuffed up someones arse. Da bomb.

25 Squid/eightf

EVEN IF U DON'T LIKE DIS BOOK, AT LEAST U CAN SMOKE IT...
DERE AINT NUFFINK MORE ANNOYIN DAN SETTLIN DOWN FOR A NICE REFRESHIN BIFTA AND
FINDIN YOU IZ GOT EVERYFIN U NEED CEPT JUST A LITTLE BIT OFF CARD FOR DA ROACH.
TO SAVE U IN DIS SITUATION FROM AVIN TO TEAR UP SOMEFIN U'D RATHER NOT, LIKE YOUR
PASSPORT (WHICH LETS BE HONEST, WE IZ ALL DONE), I IZ DONE DIS PAGE AS ROACHEZ FOR
U TO CUT OUT WHEN U NEED DEM.

STANDARD ROACH FOR EVERYDAY USE

USE DESE BIG ROACHEZ FOR SPECIAL OCCASIONZ LIKE BIRFDAYS, CHRISTMAS AND EVENINS.

indoor
gardening ©

3 SQUID$

HOW TO GROW YOUR OWN HOMEGROWN

Ali G

PLUS where 2 get the best seedz

How to grow your own homegrown

Altho in Brittun it iz now illegal to grow massive big fields of skunk like dey do in Jamaica and other parts of Africa, de law permitz u to grow up to ten plants in da privacy of your own home. Ere iz how to do it.

STEP 1: seedz

First off all u will need some seedz. Seedz iz like little eggs made of wood dat da plants live inside off. Everyfin in da world iz made of seedz – even us. Me and u woz both grown from human seedz – or as dey iz medically known "spunk".

STEP 2 : mud

Seedz dont just grow into plants on dere own – to do dis dey has to eat a special type of food, called mud. Mud iz fossilized dinasaur shit dat dont smell any more coz it iz hundreds of years old. Da best place to get it from iz Leacroft Park, where it is piled up on da edges of da grass. Fill up about three saucepans full of it and take it home.

STEP 3 : plantin

Once you has got your mud home, u has to put da seedz in
it. Put about ten in each saucepan and cover dem wiv
mud so dey cant escape. Da seedz iz now ready to start
eatin da mud that will turn them into plants, but as well
as food, dey also has to have somefin to drink – just like
human beins. Da best fing to give dem iz water. Dis might
seem a bit cruel, but me has tried giving dem fickshakes
like babies drink, but for some reason dey dont seem to
like dem and dey wont grow. As a speshul treat me
personally gives mine Ribena or Um Bongo.

STEP 4: growin

Da next fing u has to do is put da saucepans in a wardrobe. Dis might seem a bit cruel, but hunfortunatley
it iz da only way of makin fings legal. When me first started growin da skunk, me would just put dem in
da wardrobe and shut the door and dey kept dying off. Me couldnt work out why dis was appening, den me
fought, what would happen if me left me sista, Lakiesha, in a cupboard for a few days? As me found out
she would not grow and be very scared. So me den decided to put an electric lamp in da wardrobe wiv da
seedz so they wouldnt get scared, and sure enuff, it worked and dey started growin.

STEP 5: nurturin

All u is got to do now is go back to them every
few days and make sure they has got enuff
Ribena to drink. Soon u will see little plants
comin out of da mud.

STEP 6: harvestin

After about ten weeks your wardrobe will be
full of healfy, fully growed, top quality skunk
plants and u can start takin leafs of dem.

STEP 7: smoking

Your skunk is now ready for u to roll into a
massiv bifta and get mashed and I aint goin
to treat u like childrin by tellin u how u doz
dat, aiii.

helpline

**Halternatively if u cant be arsed
to do de above just ring me on
me mobile –**

07903 909762

**tell me how much "tea" u want
and me will harrange a home
delivry.**

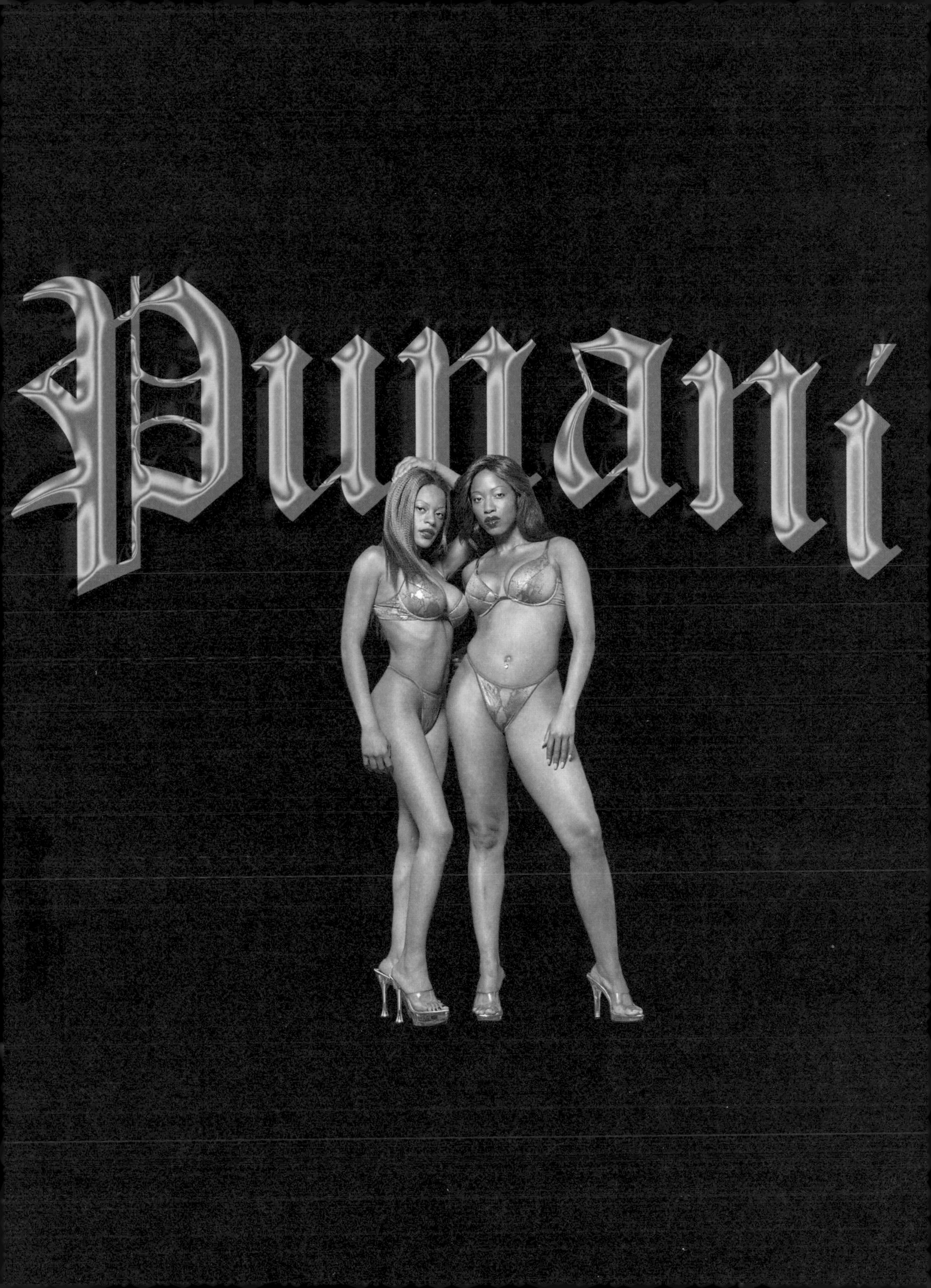
Punani

DA MIRACLE

THO MOST BABIES DESE DAYS COMES FROM ADOPTION, FOSTERIN AND DA INTRANET, IT IZ ALSO STILL POSSIBLE TO MAKE DEM THROUGH DA ACT OF BONIN. WHEN DE MAN'S SPERM JOINZ WIV DE WOMANS EGG DIS IZ CALLED DA MOMENT OF CONTRACEPTION.

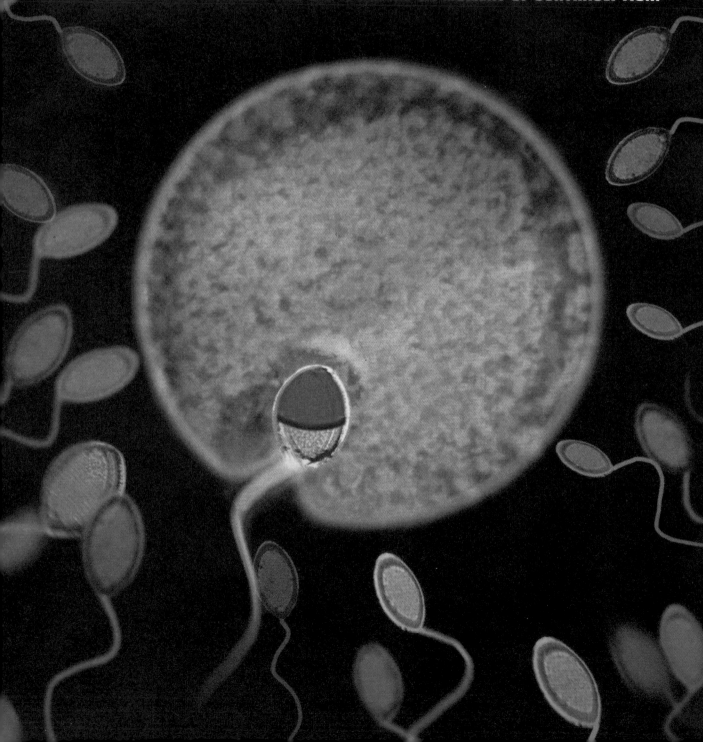

OF LIFE

IT IZ ALSO AT DIS MOMENT DAT DA SEX OF DA BABY IZ DESIDED: IF DA WOMAN IZ HAVIN A ORGASM, IT WILL BE A GIRL, IF DA MAN IZ HAVIN A ORGASM, IT WILL BE A BOY, AND IF BOTH IZ HAVIN A ORGASM, DEN IT WILL BE A GAY. FOR DIS REASON, WHEN I NOBS ME JULIE, I ALWAYS MAKES SURE DAT I COMES BEFORE SHE DO.

U MIGHT FINK IT IZ JUST A LARF BECOMIN A PARENT, BUT IT AINT – IT ALSO INVOLVE A LOT OFF VERY SERIOUS ISSUES AND RESPOSNILIBITIES INNIT. BEFORE U DO IT YOU SHOULD WAY UP DA CO'S AND PRON'S. ERE IZ A FEW FINGS U MIGHT WANT TO FINK ABOUT:

REASONZ FOR HAVIN A BABY

▷ If u has a kid, as well as bein garantteed to get a council house, da Government also pay you hextra money on top off your dole. Dis iz called Child Bennerfit and iz enuff to buy you a quarter of skunk every single week. Dis help you to bring up da kid mellow.

▷ Havin a kid mean dat u have someone to look after you when you iz old and retired in your 40s.

▷ Havin a kid iz not only a good way of hangin onto a fit woman, it also prove to everyone dat you aint a gaylord and dat your tadpoles iz well powerful.

▷ If u visit your woman in da maternity ward soon after da baby iz born, u iz likely to see a few babylons bein sucked.

▷ Most girls who babysit is well fit.

REASONZ FOR NOT HAVIN A BABY

▷ It might not be yours.

▷ It cost a lot off money. You will have to buy fings like a well loud sound system to drown out da noise off it cryin all da time.

▷ U has to buy fings for babies, but dey don't never buy u anyfin back.

▷ Havin a baby mean dat you can't nob your bitch for a few days before it iz born and even after it slips out, u may have to wait as long as 2 or 3 hours before u can start bonin again. De reason it iz dangerous to get jiggy in de last stages of pregnancy iz dat u might poke de baby in de eye wiv your beast and make him or her or it blind.

LOOKIN AFTA A PREGNANT PERSON

SOME HEXTREME FEMINISTS ARGUE DAT DE ROLE OF A FARTHER DONT JUST STOP AT GETTIN DA WOMAN PREGNANT. I AGREE WIV DEM, FARTHERS SHOOD BE INVOLVED IN DA CHILDS WELL BEIN RIGHT UP TIL DA MOMENT IT IZ BORN. SO FOLLOW DESE TIPS:

▷ A WOMAN'S DIET IZ VERY IMPORTANT – MAKE SURE SHE DOES NOT EAT QUEECHES, PRORNS, PROFITTEROLLS OR SOOSHEE – DESE IZ ONLY EATEN BY BATTYBOYS AND CONTAIN CHEMICALZ DAT MAKE PEOPLE BUM EACH OTHER.

▷ REST A LOT – A PREGNANT WOMAN SHOULDNT DO TOO MUCH FINGS LIKE HEAVY LIFTING. DA MAN SHOULD HELP AS MUCH AS HE CAN, BY CARRYING ONE OFF HER BAGS OF SHOPPING OR BRINGIN DA DUSTBINS BACK IN AFTER SHES PUT DEM OUT TO BE EMPTIED, AND FINGS LIKE DAT.

▷ LISTEN TO MUSIC – WOT A BABY HEARS WHEN IT IZ IN DA AVIARY CAN AFECT IT FOR DA REST OFF ITS LIFE, SO U MUST CHOOSE VERY CAREFULLY WOT U LISTEN TO. ME RECCOMEND HIP-HOP (EAST COAST AND WEST COAST, SO IT DON'T COME OUT PREJUDICED), SPEED GARAGE, JUNGLE AND ANYFIN ELSE DAT IZ BOTH SOOTHING AND HEDUCATIONAL. DON'T NEVER EVER EVER LET A PREGNANT PERSON NEAR INDIE MUSIC, IT IZ HACTUALLY POSSIBLE FOR BABIES TO BE INFECTED BY DIS DISEASE BEFORE DEY IZ EVEN BORN. ALSO IF YOU IZ LIVIN IN DA BARKSHIRE GHETTO, IT IZ A GOOD IDEA TO MAKE LOUD BANGS NEAR DA WOMANS BELLY TO GET DA NIPPER USED TO DA SOUND OFF GUNFIRE.

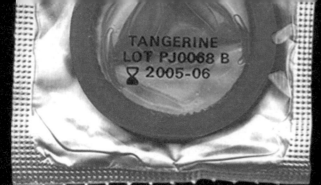

HOW NOT TO GET
YOUR WOMAN PREGNANT

COMDONS

Also known as 'connies', 'johnnies', 'sperm banks' and 'cock socks'. Girlz can buy dese from Chemists or pubs, and can find dem in da woods behind Egham cricket pavilion (dey iz as good as new). Warning: dey do reduse sensitivity durin intracorse so me personally reccomend cuttin da end off for a much more enjoyable shag. Also, it iz not hygienic to use dem more dan about 5 times each unless u put dem in da washin machine (do NOT tumble dry).

Other halternatives to connies dat do de same fing are crisp bags (not salt and vinegar – me recommend Spicy BBQ coz it leave your helmie wiv a nice aftertaste for post-noshin), clingfilm and veruca socks.

DA PILL

Da pill iz somefin invented by Lezzas in da 1860s coz dey was unable to wear connies. To be habsolutely 90% sure dey work me suggest dat blokes take dem as well.

BANANA
LOT PD0041 Q
2005-07

DA FEMMYDONG

Dis iz like a big sock made of rubber dat look like a carrier bag – in fact, wiv a lot of girls in Staines, it hactually iz a carrier bag. It go inside da punani and traps da man's giz. U has to fix it on da outside wiv some sellotape. Me personally dont like dese coz it mean dat da woman den has a bag off my giz which she could sell for millionz of squidz.

DA COIL

Da coil is a big spring dat goes inside a vadge and when a mans nob hits it, it bounces straight out again.

Finally, dis iz da most reliable form off contraception of all. Nuff said.

GETTIN JIGGY WID IT

DA PUNANI IS ONE OF DA MOST AMAZIN FINGS DAT JAH HAS EVER CREATED ALONG WIV KFC AND JACKIE CHAN. DA WAY IT FEEL, DA WAY IT LOOK (AFTER A VISIT TO PINK CHEEKS IN EGHAM) AND WHAT IT REPREZENT TO DA HOLE RACE OF HUMAN BEANS, MAKE IT DA GREATEST GIFT FOR A MAN DAT DERE IZ EVER BEEN.

DRINKIN FROM DE FURRY CUP

WHILE AT DA EARLY STAGES OF A RELASHUNSHIP U IZ PROBABLY UP FOR EATING FROM DE BUSHY PLATE. AFTER ABOUT A WEEK U PROBLY CANNOT BE ARSED TO DO IT ANYMORE – AFTER ALL WOT PLEAZURE DOES IT BRING TO U? DAT IZ WHY U MUST MEMORIZE DE FOLLOWING:

5 EXCUSES TO AVOID GOIN DOWNTOWN

1. U IZ SO BEAUTIFUL DAT ME WANNA SEE YOUR FACE
2. IT IZ ILLEGAL AT DA MOMENT COS OF DA OUTBREAK OF FANNY AND MOUTH DISEASE
3. ME HAZ JUST PUT IN A NEW GOLD TOOF AND ME DONT WANT IT TO RUST
4. U IZ GOT DE PAINTERS IN AND ME DONT WANT 2 GET A TASTE FOR IT, IN CASE I IZ A VAMPIRE
5. I IZ GOT A COLD AND ME DONT WANT TO GIVE U FANNY FLU
6. ME HAS JUST HAD SOME RED WINE, AND U DONT AVE TO BE JAMIE HOLIVER TO KNOW DAT RED WINE AND FISH DONT MIX

Da JOY of Bonin

Da most detailed luvvaz guide ever writtun

Not many people know dis but dere iz more dan two positions dat u can have sex in. Dat iz why to help u thru da confusion of sexual intracourses me has provided u wiv a step by step guide of how to do it in interestin positionz for lovin couples.

HOW TO DO 'IT' IN DA BOGS IN KFC

Da bogs at da Egham branch of KFC iz typical of your average KFC bog and so me will use dem as me template.

1. Sit yourself down on da seat and make yourself comfie as if droppin a massive shit. (NB do not hactually drop one – coz dis iz not romantic). Put down some bog roll beneath your batty to act as a barrier against disease.
2. Spray some of de air freshener to create a romantic atmosfere. Make sure de door iz locked.
3. If de manager knocks on de door and says 'wot iz u doin in dere?', convinse him dat u iz in dere for official purposes by squeezin out a guff and if she iz able, let her accompany u wiv a punani fart.
4. Let her lower her bargain bucket onto your drumstick as she holds onto da coat hook. I call dis position da 'Chikken Dipper'.

HOW TO DO 'IT' IN DA BACK OFF A RENAULT 5
(2 DOOR HATCHBACK)

1. Park in a deserted place – like behind de Elmsleigh Shoppin Centre or dat road next to de playin fields by Cranleigh Gardens – u know de one wiv de mini-roundabout. Do not park outside number 43, becoz de geeza who lives dere iz head of his Neighbourhood Watch which include watchin u and ya missus getting jiggy thru his video camera.

2. Put on some romantic music to get her in da mood. Me recommend Jungle Anthems – Sound of de Underground 6, or Probably de Best Jungle Album Ever 8.

3. Position her batty over de subwoofers – at moments of extreme bass de vibrations will stimulate her poony.

4. Wind back de seats to allow more room for bumpin and grindin.

5. Be careful not to hit de hooter during extreme batty movement.

6. Lie down on de seat. Den get de lady to posishun herself on top of u, supportin herself by holdin on to dat strange andle above de door – now u now why every single car has dem.

7. Ladies should use deir other hand for balance, by holding on to de gearstick. But make sure she do not mistake de handbreak for your beast, becoz when she finks she iz pullin u off de car will roll bakwards, smash into a phone box and corrs 852 squidz worth of damage, which den de insurance sudenly say dey wont cover, coz u has only paid for '3rd party, fire and theft' and not for '3rd party, fire, theft and bonin'.

HOW TO BONE IN DE ABC CINEMA IN STAINES

1. Buy tickets for de loudest film posible – either a film about dinosaurs or lorries.

2. Do NOT buy tickets for de back row. Dat iz wear everyone iz expectin u to bone and some of de seats dere iz already covered in giz (I personaly has 'tagged' seat 14). Instead go right for de front saying dat u need hextra 'legroom'. If anyone sees u ere, dey will fink u iz part of de film.

3. Make sure u iz facin de screen so dat u do not miss any of de film.

4. Buy a large tub of popcorn. Once u has sat down, make a hole on de bottom of de tub about an inch wide and den stick your beast thru it.

5. Den get de lady to put her hand in de tub and search for de best bit of popcorn. She should continue doin dis for about 5 minutes. Make sure u has not bought salty popcorn coz dey will sting your japseye. Anywayz if all goes to plan, de popcorn will becum salty anyway, aiii.

6. Try not to let out your soldiers until a particalarly scary bit of da film. Dat way people will fink u iz well excited about lorries and not just spunkin up.

7. After about an hour do not forget wot has happened and start munchin on de popcorn again.

Bitches I has Boned

I aint tryin to show off or nuffin, but I has done it wiv all de followin girls. Ere iz just a few memories of some of de romances I iz had.

It woz me Destiny 2 bone dem

j-Blo

she woz in Langley Village 4 da weekend —we hooked up-den dis happenend

Problemz

It iz sometimes embarassin to talk about sex let alone sexual problemz. Sumfin dat effex a lot of blokes iz premature ejaculation. By de way dis does not efect me, not at all. If u iz tried medical treatments and your solgerz iz still leavin de trenchez 2 early, den me has de perfect cure. Please turn owver de page.

Pull dis photo out of de book and stick it above your bed. Me guarantee it will give u at least anuvver 10 minitz

GET INVOLVED IN YA FUTURE

U CANNOT JUST SIT ON YOUR BATTY AT HOME WATCHIN GRANADA MEN AND MOTORS, PARTICULARLY COZ DE SWINGAZ ONLY COME OUT AFTER 11.

U MUST TRY AND CHANGE DE WORLD AND MAKE IT DE MOST BESTEST PLACE DAT IT CAN BE. DAT IZ WHY IT IZ YOUR DUTY TO BECUM POLITICALY ACTIVE – I AINT TALKIN BOUT VOTING. U AINT NEVER GONNA CHANGE DE GOVENMENT LIKE DAT. AND RIOTZ, WHILE DEY IZ A WIKID LARF, DON'T APPEN DAT OFTEN.

WHY SHOULD U CHANGE DE WORLD?

U SHOULD DO IT 4 YOUR CHUILDRENS BENEFIT... AND FOR YOUR UNEMPLOYMENT BENEFIT, YOUR HOUSING BENEFIT AND YOUR DISABILITY BENEFIT – TRY TO INCREAS DEM AS MUCH AS POSIBLE.

ERE IZ A LETTER I IZ RITTEN FOR U, JUST STICK YOUR NAME AT DE BOTTOM AND SEND IT OF.

I KNOW IT'S A DREAM BUT TOGETHER LETS TRY AND MAKE DE PLACE WHERE WE BRING UP OUR KIDZ TO BE AS GOOD AS SOUTH CENTRAL LA.

```
                                        10 Drowning Street
                                         De White House
                                          London
                                          England
                                          De world
                                          De universe
                                        De Milky Way
                                         De Finger of Fudge
```

Dear President Blairs,

Me hope dat u and ya missus ~~Cherell~~ Cheryl iz well and dat she aint up
da duff again. If she iz den pleaz den send her my best and me hope dat dis
time it will be yourz. By da way your son Ewen rings me~~allmost~~ almost
every week. Tell him he aint getting no more until he pays up for de
last batch. After all it don't grow on trees - it growz on plants.
I has folowed your time in office carefuly and has come to de folowin ~~konklushun~~
conklusion. I fink u are shit. Dats why I iz rightin to u so
dat u can make yourself less crap. Listenup fool:

1. Stop bein racialist - even tho u iz de ~~prime~~ ~~minister~~ president of dis
country u iz made habsolutely no effort to be black.   U has not tried to
make any token friends wiv bruvvas and me mate Ricky C saw u makin faces
and doin dem rabbit ear fings behind Nelson Mandela's head. Dat weren't
very nice or fu~~nnnnnx~~ funny.

2.   U iz been in govement for 11 yearz now an u still aint legalized hash
- how long does it take? Why iz it dat it iz legal in EVERY other
country in de world and not ere? Aint it ~~hypo~~ ~~hypo~~ hypocriticalist dat
hash iz illegal, but Pringles whitch iz well known to be de most
addictive drug out dere iz legal? I iz sure u knows deir 'advertisin'
slogan 'once you pop you cannot stop'. Open your eyez Blairz or iz u
blind? Oh no dat's de ovver other one innit.

3. Why don't u   increas benefit to single mothers? Dat way dey will not
be so scared bout gettin another bun in da oven and so consequenshaly be
less frigid.

Yours unfaithfully

- - - - - - - - - - - - - - - -

(put ya name)

Da End

I HOPE U HAS ENJOYED READIN DIS BOOK MUCH MORE DAN I HAS ENJOYED WRITIN IT – IT IZ BEEN A FUCKIN HASSLE. NEVERDELESS ME HOPE IT HAS TAUGHT US BOTH A LOT – U DE WAY TO LIVE A HAPPY AN FULFILLIN LIFE, AND ME NEVER TO WRITE A STINKIN BOOK AGAIN. ANYWAYZ, FANK U FOR BUYIN OR HOPEFULLY EVEN NICKIN DIS BOOK. GO OUT, FINK ABOUT DE MEANING OF DE WORDZ, HEXPLORE DE DEEPA ISSUES AND DEN PERHAPS KNOCK ONE OUT OVER DE MANY KWALITY PICTURES I IZ PROVIDED U WIV - I KNOW I CERTAINLY HAS.

Respect ya Nan
Peace